INDUSTRIAL POLICY:
THE FIXITIES HYPOTHESIS

Industrial Policy: The Fixities Hypothesis

Policy Study Series

Ontario Economic Council

Christopher Green

Canadian Cataloguing in Publication Data

Green, Christopher, 1937—
    Industrial policy: the fixities hypothesis

(Policy study series/Ontario Economic Council,
ISSN 0227-0005)
Bibliography: p.
ISBN 0-7743-9362-9

1. Industry and State – Canada.   2. Canada – Economic
policy. I. Ontario Economic Council. II. Title. III. Series:
Policy study series (Ontario Economic Council)

HD3619.C3G7 1984   338.971   84-093017-8

Christopher Green is a professor of economics at McGill University.

This report reflects the views of the author and not necessarily those of the
Ontario Economic Council. The Council establishes policy questions to be
investigated and commissions research projects, but it does not influence
the conclusions or recommendations of authors. The decision to sponsor
publication of this study was based on its competence and relevance to public
policy and was made with the advice of anonymous referees expert in the area.

Contents

Acknowledgements

A number of people were very helpful to me at various stages in the work on this monograph. I am particularly indebted to Professor Richard M. Bird, who read each of the drafts, for many insights, references, and modifications, most of which were incorporated into the manuscript, and for vital encouragement when it was most needed. The role of the Institute for Policy Analysis of the University of Toronto in organizing and facilitating the preparation of this study is greatly appreciated. William G. Watson and Ronald S. Saunders also read drafts of the manuscript and made many valuable suggestions. I had useful conversations with my colleague Paul Davenport and with William G. Milne, and I received helpful comments from Lok Ho and two anonymous referees. I am also indebted to Cathy Duggan for typing each draft of the manuscript and to Lenore d'Anjou for expert editing of the final text. Any remaining errors are the responsibility of the author.

1
Introduction

Since the Great Depression of the 1930s, a tide of government intervention has risen in the Canadian economy, as in most industrialized economies.[1] One wave takes the form of stabilization policies, social insurance and income redistribution, the provision of collective and other public goods, and the control of externalities such as pollution – programs now considered essential to the healthy operation of a modern industrial society. Also sweeping over the economy, however, is a flood of direct government intervention in individual firms and commodity and factor markets. These interventions take many forms: regulations, firm-specific and industry-wide subsidies, quotas and other kinds of nontariff barriers, procurement policies, government ownership, tax expenditures and incentives, and so on. These policies, which this study terms 'interventionist industrial policies',[2] have increased in number and extent and now make up the bulk of what are sometimes called 'public policies towards business' (to distinguish them from government's public finance function[3]).

The explanations for the growth of interventionist industrial policies in Canada are numerous. Davenport et al. (1982) recently outlined several hypotheses involving causal factors as diverse as an increased concern with market failure, a renewal of Canada's historical national policy of protecting its economic and political identity, a response to domestic stagflation and external economic shocks, the federal-provincial tug-of-war over economic and other powers, and rent-seeking and rent-maintaining behaviour by the prospective beneficiaries.

No doubt each of these hypotheses has at least some explanatory power. This study suggests the importance of yet another factor: the existence of what I call 'fixities' – individual or household assets that are difficult or impossible to transfer or transport and hence make labour-mobility responses to economic change difficult, costly, and potentially inconsistent with maximizing behaviour by households.

2   Industrial policy: the fixities hypothesis

As we explore the content and ramifications of the fixities hypothesis, it is important to remember that the aim of the study is to help explain the growth of interventionist industrial policies in Canada. The hypothesis entertained here is at best one of a number of partial explanations for increasing government intervention in individual private-sector markets. Here I ask questions others have in similar contexts. Why is intervention demanded, and why is it supplied? What economic changes have led to an increasing call for government protection of or assistance to individual firms and industries? Is something inherent in economic change that makes interventionist policies virtually inevitable, if not healthy or desirable?

As already noted, one convincing set of explanations for the extent and growth of government intervention in the Canadian marketplace focusses on nationalist and protectionist reactions to the facts of the country's small population, large geographic size, and proximity to the economic giant to the south. These demographic-geographic factors contribute to a small, loosely linked domestic economy and polity that, it is alleged, are especially susceptible to foreign influence and identity loss in the absence of protectionist-nationalist policies. Another explanation is that intervention is sought by narrow-based interest groups seeking individual or private gain and supplied by vote-seeking legislators operating in a pluralistic democracy. In contrast, this study asks whether something in economic progress itself naturally increases the demand for interventionist industrial policies – a demand that, for political reasons, evokes a supply response, even if one is ill-advised.

At this point the reader must avoid falling into a possible trap. My study is positive in nature: it attempts to explain what is. It is not a normative study; it does not address the issue of what ought to be. Even if the argument in this study persuades readers, neither they nor I have any basis for concluding that interventionist industrial policies are desirable. Nothing in logic implies that what is is what ought to be. I will leave the reader to reach his or her own normative judgements. However, I should warn that I view the world paradoxically. While I think it quite possible that our very affluence has contributed to the growth of interventionist industrial policies, I am also inclined to believe that widespread intervention is likely to kill the goose that lays the golden egg.

Industrial policy: two views of demand and supply
The issues this study tackles can best be attacked by distinguishing two views about the demand for and supply of industrial policies. Before doing

so, it is useful to consider the concepts of rent-seeking and rent-maintaining behaviour.

Rent-seeking involves the investment in and use of resources by interest groups or coalitions to obtain from government special advantages, typically in the form of protection from competition (for example, minimum prices, entry controls, and/or output quotas), exclusive rights, or subsidies. The goal is to obtain an increase (or avoid a decrease) in income or wealth by altering legal rights.[4] Rent-maintaining, on the other hand, is activity designed to protect existing income or wealth. In a way, it is a subset of rent-seeking activity in which the object is to secure positions or advantages already held, including the maintenance of normal returns on investments in human and nonhuman capital. Thus, rent-seeking and rent-maintaining may end in similar behaviour. Nevertheless, they may differ in causes and goals and sometimes also in results and principal actors.

In the case at hand, focussing on one sort of behaviour or the other may lead analysts to subtly different interpretations of the nature of the demand for and supply of industrial policies. The analyst who emphasizes rent-seeking will say that many of these policies are sought by their prospective beneficiaries and supplied by a political process in which campaign funds, electoral legwork, and single-issue voting are paramount. Such a view underlies Stigler's (1971) cartelization theory (see also Jordan's [1972] producer-protection theory) of economic regulation. Stigler casts the decision to regulate in terms of economic behaviour, emphasizing the use of the political process by organized groups of economic agents seeking to appropriate a larger share of the surplus (consumer and producer) generated by economic activity. Specifically, interest groups demand regulation, and politicians and civil servants supply it.[5] The theory of cartels provides the underpinning for the demand side of Stigler's theory. Political support by identifiable blocs combines with the log-rolling process to supply the needed majorities in a pluralistic democracy. In this view, regulation is a reflection of private rather than public interest: it benefits certain individuals or groups, particularly in their role as producers, rather than all members of the community in their role as consumers.

Another view is that some industrial policies are a reaction to economic hardship and are supplied by politicians and civil servants who feel obliged to act – in the most practical, if not the most economically efficient, manner to maintain the economic status quo.[6] This view, which I term the 'response-to-economic-exigency' hypothesis, resembles the 'economic-due-process' theory of regulation put forth by Owen and Braeutigam (1978). They point out that the market under a regime of competition can be 'ruthless' in its treatment of specific individuals or groups. It is not a matter of class but of much smaller subsets of society who find themselves on the losing end of shifting preferences and technological changes. Owen and Braeutigam speculate that protective regulations – to which we may add other forms of industrial and occupational assistance – may be in good part a social response to inexorable economic changes: government attempts to maintain normal returns on those private investments in human and nonhuman capital that the 'ruthless efficiency of the market' would, in the absence of intervention, unexpectedly erode to below-normal or negative levels (Owen and Braeutigam 1978, 20-1). In other words, the very efficiency of the market generates resistance to its operation.[7]

These two views are obviously not mutually exclusive. Both are subsumed in Courchene's concern that the increase in government intervention entails, as he subtitled a recent paper, 'The politicization of economic life'. On one hand, organized interest groups turn to the political process for protection from competition. On the other, economic exigency stimulates endangered groups to seek aid and protection, and the democratic process may force elected representatives to respond even if that response is against their better judgement. In each case, the political behaviour is the same. Nevertheless, the two views are based on different assessments of what stimulates economic agents to engage in political behaviour.

In other words, the underlying distinction between the two views is that the former relies on a rent-seeking theory (see Buchanan, Tollison, and Tullock 1981) of political behaviour with monopoly rents as the prize, while the latter focusses on the response to unrequited capital losses – or the prospect of such losses – that economic change inevitably creates for some individuals and groups, even within a growing capitalist system.[8]

The present study
This study probes a version of the second view.[9] Specifically, it examines the response to the economic exigency produced by economic change that results in a sharp decline in the value of some human or nonhuman capital.

The impact of economic change on market values is particularly acute when the assets involved are specific to location (nonportable) and/or to individuals (nontransferable). In these cases, the threatened individuals or groups can be expected to try to use political institutions and processes to gain a degree of protection and thus maintain the value of their capital. Thus, the main hypothesis of this study is that at least some of the apparent growth in interventionist industrial policies is a political response to the sort of economic exigency that is produced when adverse economic change threatens the value of nonportable, nontransferable assets – what I call 'fixities'.

The study proceeds as follows. Chapter 2 assesses the role of economic change and the response to it, using Hirschman's (1970) exit-voice framework to distinguish the economic (mobility) response from the political (organized-action) response to prospective change. Chapter 3 focusses on the mobility response, citing the determinants of geographic mobility as well as various barriers to it. The fixities hypothesis and its theoretical underpinnings are presented in Chapter 4, in which the concept of fixities in household production functions is explained and assessed, and in Chapter 5, where the analysis is extended to provincial and local governments.

The empirical side of the study appears in Chapters 6, 7, and 8. Chapter 6 presents evidence that fixities in household production functions have grown along with the growth in household wealth. Chapter 7 shows that fixities have influenced individual behaviour; because there is no obvious data base on which to test the fixities hypothesis, five brief case studies are used as evidence. Some evidence of the possible influence of fixities on government behaviour in moulding industrial policies is offered in Chapter 8. A summary and a conclusion appear in Chapter 9.

The study breaks no new ground in the normative analysis of industrial policies, a subject on which there is already plenty of useful work. Recent studies by Usher (1982) and Watson (1983), for example, provide excellent discussions of the basis for economists' traditional skepticism about industrial policies. As a starting point, I accept their view that widespread intervention in the marketplace produces undesirable economic effects and poses political dangers as well.[10] However, I am also persuaded that the standard welfare-theoretic analysis of government intervention uses too static a context and hence inadequately reflects the world of continuing economic and technological change. Moreover, it usually fails to capture the historical and institutional framework within which intervention takes place and which matters a great deal to politicians and voters.[11] Yet people are generally reluctant to accept the case against a policy unless they understand, and can therefore reject, the rationale for implementing it in the first place.

2
The response to economic change

In a classic paper Hayek (1945) argues that:

The peculiar character of the problem of a rational economic order is determined precisely by the fact that the knowledge of the circumstances of which we must make use never exists in concentrated or integrated form, but solely as the dispersed bits of incomplete and frequently contradictory knowledge which all separate individuals possess. The economic problem of society is thus not merely a problem of how to allocate 'given' resources – it is a problem of the utilization of knowledge not given to anyone in its totality. (519-20)

The knowledge to which Hayek refers is not 'scientific knowledge' but knowledge of the 'particular circumstances of time and place'. The 'economic problem' here 'arise[s] always and only as a consequence of change' and requires 'rapid adaptation to changes in the particular circumstances of time and place' (Hayek 1945, 523-4). On the basis of these premises, Hayek made his well-known case against central planning and for a decentralized system of decision-making by individuals, the people most familiar with the particular circumstances of time and place. Paradoxically, the same argument can be used both to make a case against industrial policy-making (which is, in many respects, a mild form of central planning) and to explain why government action is so much in demand.

The heart of the economic problem is, as Hayek states, adjustment to continuous and increasingly rapid economic change. It may well be, as Hayek argues, that from the standpoint of knowledge the individual has the fastest reflexes and is thereby in the best position when it comes to adjusting to economic change. But that position does not necessarily make adjustment easy or costless. For the individual or group adversely affected by economic change, it may make sense to devote time and other resources to resisting it – to trying to slow, soften, or halt it – rather than simply to adjust to something that produces unrequited capital losses.

Short of Luddite-type violence against new technology, resistance to economic change generally requires the use of political tools and the political process. Thus, at one level, Hayek's economic analysis is incomplete: although the individual may be in the best position to adjust to economic change, he or she may be unwilling to accept the consequences of adjustment and so may organize with other losers to resist it, using the available political institutions. For this reason, Hayek (1960) is forced to complement his economic analysis with a political one that places constitutional limits on the capacity of organized economic groups to use the political process to their own private advantage (see also Grubel 1982). In the absence of such limits, decentralized, individual decision-making, no matter how great its efficacy, provides no assurance that individuals will not ask the state to intervene in the market economy or that the state will not respond. Ultimately, the investigation of industrial policy cannot be divorced from an analysis of individual utility-maximizing (or cost-minimizing) behaviour.

THE CAPITALIST DYNAMIC: WINNERS AND LOSERS

What are the institutional and historical facts that matter here? The following summary is highly stylized but perhaps not a gross oversimplification. Capitalist economic systems are intrinsically dynamic: they undergo continuous but erratic economic change.[1] In the process they produce winners *and* losers. Even if a system is growing rapidly and real wages are rising (Viner 1960), even if a change greatly benefits society as a whole, there are invariably losers. The reason is that the socially efficient response to economic change usually requires resource movement – geographical, occupational, industrial, hierarchical. Most such movement is time-consuming and involves information, transactions, and moving costs. The losers must also bear capital losses as well as reductions in factor returns per unit of time. The consequence is individual or group resistance to change, which is as much a reflection of maximizing behaviour as it is of conservatism or lethargy. In other words, microeconomics' timeless and frictionless model of optimal resource allocation fails to capture essential institutional facts that have important behavioural implications.[2]

The capitalist dynamic can be quantified. Take, for example, the turnover of firms and plants. New ones appear, old ones are closed down. Table 1 gives us some information about the magnitude of this dynamic process. Of the firms and plants that accounted for almost all Canada's employment in and output from manufacturing and mining in 1970, about a quarter had disappeared by 1976. However, an approximately equal

TABLE 1
Openings and closings in manufacturing and mining, 1970–6

	Firms	Plants	% of total output	Employment (000s)
All Canada				
Total in existence, 1970[a]	17,079	21,798	[a]	1,914.0
Openings[b]	4,211	4,641	9.3[d]	162.8
Closings[c]	4,657	5,230	7.9[e]	169.3
Net change, 1970–6	-446	-589		-6.5
Ontario				
Total, 1970[a]	6,857	8,673	[a]	–
Openings[b]	1,558	1,678	6.6[d]	–
Closings[c]	1,675	1,874	6.5[c]	–
Net change, 1970–6	-117	-196		–
Quebec				
Total in existence, 1970[a]	6,758	7,616	[a]	–
Openings[b]	1,539	1,610	10.2[d]	–
Closings[c]	1,929	2,019	9.3[e]	–
Net change, 1970–6	-390	-409		–

[a] The survey included approximately 70 per cent of all enterprises and establishments. These accounted for 98 per cent of total manufacturing and mining output.
[b] Defined as either the opening of a newly constructed plant or the transfer into manufacture or mining of an existing plant from another sector.
[c] Defined as either the closing of a plant or the transfer of one to another sector.
[d] As a percentage of the value of manufacturing and mining production in 1976.
[e] As a percentage of the value of manufacturing and mining production in 1970.
SOURCE: Canada (1981b), tables I, XVIII, 5, and pp. 16, 68, 72, 103, 104.

number were born during the same period, so the *net* loss was less that 3 per cent.[3] The resultant *net* change in employment was also small for Canada as a whole and was presumably so for Ontario and Quebec too. (Statistics on employment change at the provincial-regional level were not published.)

Nevertheless, this essentially efficient process of turnover clearly produces winners *and* losers. Not least of the losers are the many workers who find themselves out of jobs, often with their investments in homes and pension plans in jeopardy, when plants close.

APPLYING THE 'EXIT-VOICE' FRAMEWORK

How does an economic agent select an appropriate (utility-maximizing or cost-minimizing) response to change? The economic theorist presumes that any appropriate response is a market response: consumer mobility among products, location, and so on. Hirschman (1970) calls this response 'exit' and shows that both an alternative and a complement to it exist in 'voice' – the use of the political process.

Hirschman's 'exit-voice' framework can be directly applied to the issues raised in this study. In the face of change that affects them adversely, economic agents have a choice between 'exit' and 'voice'. 'Exit' is accomplished by politically neutral moves of resources from one use to another; 'voice' is politically non-neutral behaviour by economic agents who would rather stick than switch and call upon their political representatives for help.

Which route will economic agents choose in response to events over which they may have little or no control? Let us distinguish between *ex post* and *ex ante* responses. There is often little that one can do after the fact. Having lost, the loser must accept the losses. Social insurance benefits – for example, unemployment compensation for the job loser – may soften the blow. In general, however, the main support for losers comes from the goodwill or self-interest of winners, who in a wealthy society are unlikely to stand by and see some of its members suffer large losses as a result of adverse economic change. Such help is usually proffered through the agency of government programs (rather than through private charity) in the form of either regular income-maintenance payments or market-intervening industrial policies.

Ex ante responses are more interesting. To help protect themselves against future adversity, economic agents may take out insurance if it is available, or they may band together with others who face similar risks in an attempt to control the market, the institution through which most economic changes are fed. Since the insurance route is often fraught with problems – insurers face the dangers of moral hazard, and the cost to the insured may be high – economic agents may prefer to organize if the costs of doing so are not too great. Trade unions, professional associations, marketing boards, and trade associations are obvious examples of horizontal organizations whose objective is, in one way or another, a degree of market control.

Market control can be attempted directly (which is generally illegal under the anti-combines laws) or indirectly by lobbying for protective government legislation. In a democratic society, political institutions from parliaments to regulatory boards are often sensitive to the persuasion of organized groups, particularly to arguments that they be given at least some protection from economic adversity. In practical politics, this sensitivity is generally aided by a log-rolling process, which is virtually inevitable in a pluralistic society with no constitutional restraints on the substance of economic legislation.[4]

Thus, the economic theorist's emphasis on mobility as the response to economic change is too simplistic. 'Exit' not only involves moving costs; it may also mean capital losses. *Ex post*, the acceptance of losses may be inevitable; *ex ante*, it is not. Thus, well before change makes 'exit' necessary, we can expect economic agents to take precautions to ensure that losses will be minimized and security maximized.

CONCLUSION

Whether it is rent-seeking behaviour or economic exigency that gives rise to a demand for government intervention in markets, the exit-voice framework can help to explain the political element in the growth of industrial policies. In either case, 'voice' is the mechanism employed in getting government to act.

3
Mobility and economic change

One could argue that in our increasingly democratic and affluent society, the use of 'voice', the political response, has increased relative to the use of 'exit', the economic response of mobility. Neoclassical economic theory, however, puts a premium on the movement of resources seeking out their most productive and remunerative uses. Presumably, the more rapid the economic change, the greater the pressure on resources to move from one employment to another.

Given the importance of mobility to the operation of the market, let us examine the phenomenon more closely. The focus here, as elsewhere in this study, is on the geographic mobility of labour.

GEOGRAPHIC MOBILITY

Perhaps as a reflection of the importance of change in modern economic life, the determinants of occupational, industrial, and geographic mobility have received increasing attention in recent years. Although the factors affecting geographic mobility are complex, most analyses have followed the human-capital approach, which emphasizes the role of economic determinants in the migration decision (Greenwood 1975). Even socio-demographic factors, such as education and age, have economic aspects, which are reflected in the increase in lifetime earnings that a worker can expect to achieve from migration. Empirical studies confirm that economic factors, in the form of earnings differentials and the probability of acquiring and retaining employment, significantly influence a household's decision to move from one locale to another (Courchene 1974; Vanderkamp and Grant 1976; Fields 1979; Winer and Gauthier 1982).

History is full of examples of sizeable migrations induced by the availability of jobs. In the United States, for instance, the mechanization of southern agriculture, especially cotton-growing, displaced large numbers of agricultural labourers, who were ultimately forced to move north to find employment. Again, in recent years, industrial growth in the southern and southwestern US, where relatively cheap and secure energy is to be found, has induced a movement of labour away from declining industrial areas in the northeast and midwest.

Mobility is, of course, a two-way street; jobs also move to people. In other words, neoclassical theory includes not only labour adjustment but also capital adjustment by movement into locations and fields of endeavour in which substantial pools of labour exist. Many instances of this phenomenon also exist. For example, during the early twentieth century, many US textile mills were moved from New England into the upper south, where there were large pools of unorganized workers willing to accept low wages. Years later high-technology industries moved into New England, where there were large numbers of trained workers. In Canada, until recently, a combination of cultural factors (primarily language, rapid population growth, and workers' willingness to accept lower-than-average wages) made Quebec a natural location for the relatively labour-intensive and low-productivity clothing and textile industries.

Notwithstanding the case of the textile and clothing industries, the main emphasis in Canada, with its relatively sparse population spread over a huge, resource-rich land base, has been on the movement of people to jobs. Capital and jobs are located where markets are close at hand, close to the US border and population centres, or where resources are found. Thus, the resource-poor parts of the hinterland have lost population to the metropolitan and resource-rich regions. No small part of Canada's industrial policy has been intended to stem this population flow by inducing a reverse flow of capital, often in the form of Department of Regional Economic Expansion (DREE) grants and equalization payments.

The determinants of mobility
What factors influence the choice of jobs' moving to people or people's moving to jobs? I have already suggested two: the relative abundance or scarcity of resources and the degree to which an industry is market oriented. Another factor is the flexibility of wages. In the case of the US textile industry, for example, capital flowed to a region where wages were lower and potentially flexible downward. In Canada, however, many intra-industry wages do not vary significantly on a geographic basis.[1] Strong unions and legislated minimum wages in Canada have largely eliminated the relative wage inducement for capital to flow to regions with pools of unemployed or underemployed labour. Moreover, even if not totally rigid, wage rates are surely sticky downward, and strong unions

have often prevented a wage rather than employment response to industry decline.[2]

Barriers to mobility
Another set of factors may inhibit the tendency of people to move to jobs. These are various barriers to the movement of labour between regions or provinces.

The barriers to the geographic mobility of labour can be classified as natural or artificial. Among the latter, one can distinguish between barriers established for the specific purpose of protecting home workers from the competition of migrants and barriers that are institutionally inherent in a program or set of rules but accidentally influence migration decisions.

Table 2 is a taxonomy of mobility barriers, using some admittedly arbitrary distinctions. The natural barriers are the pecuniary and non-pecuniary factors that make moving economically or psychologically costly. As for the artificial barriers that are institutionally inherent, some are well known, including seniority rules and rigid wages. Less obvious are

TABLE 2
A taxonomy of barriers to mobility

Motivation	Type	
	Natural	Artificial
None: barrier is institutionally inherent	Moving or relocation costs Higher costs of living in region where workers are needed most Home ownership in a thin housing market Nonpecuniary preference for remaining in a particular locale Jobs of other family members in home locale Language	Vesting provisions in private pension plans Income tax structure Seniority rules Rigid wages
To protect home labour force		Hiring-hall practices of some unions Restrictions on transferability of trade and professional certification Language laws Preferential hiring laws

private pension plans – their lack of portability, vesting regulations, and 'lock-in' provisions whereby a worker cannot withdraw contributions – which have a potentially dampening impact on worker mobility (Rea and Pesando 1980).[3]

The last category is artificial barriers, those established to protect home labour or existing union or professional membership. Well-known examples include Quebec provisions that make difficult the employment of nonresident construction workers, regulations that give preference to Newfoundlanders in that province's burgeoning petroleum industry, provinces' refusal to recognize the professional and apprenticeship certifications of other provinces, and hiring-hall preferences for local union membership. Though such practices are the most flagrant barriers to mobility and have come under attack as contributing to the balkanization of Canada (*Globe and Mail*, 8 March 1982, p. 8), they are not necessarily the most important.

CONCLUSION

Mobility is a phenomenon of great complexity, even if one focusses solely on the geographic mobility of labour. Economic theory predicts that if capital does not move to pools of labour, labour will adjust by moving to the location of jobs, and this phenomenon has certainly occurred in Canada, as elsewhere. Various factors may, however, discourage workers from moving, even if doing so would seem to offer clear economic advantages in terms of higher lifetime earnings and an increased probability of obtaining and retaining employment.

Some of these barriers, including many of those I have classified as artificial, have received considerable attention from analysts and even the public media. Yet they are not necessarily the most important. In the following chapters, I propose that the very growth in household affluence, reflected in an increase in assets of all kinds, may be both a more subtle and a more important factor than those that have received the most public attention to date.

4
The fixities hypothesis: the household production function

With the sustained growth that followed the Great Depression came an important change in the economic landscape. Household wealth rose dramatically, an increase only partially mirrored in the increase in real per-capita GNP reported in the national income accounts. Household wealth takes many forms – human and nonhuman, financial and non-financial, status- and nonstatus-related – so its composition, as well as its size, may change over time. It accumulates as the result of past investments in human and nonhuman capital and of time-related attainments of economic status, such as those represented by seniority rights and job tenure.

As we shall see, the significance of the growth in household wealth and its changing composition resides in two characteristics of many household assets:

– Their market values are often sensitive to economic change.
– In many cases they are specific to location or to individuals and are thereby nonportable and/or nontransferable.[1] In other cases, portability and/or transferability may be technically possible but very difficult or costly.

It is the existence of asset-specificity, which I have termed 'fixity', in household and government production functions that may make economic mobility particularly costly and difficult.[2]

While it is true that people often refuse to move for noneconomic reasons – family, cultural, linguistic, aesthetic – the fixities hypothesis provides an explanation for immobility in terms of economic, utility-maximizing behaviour.[3] That is, the theory does not rely on taste factors to explain immobility in the face of economic exigency. Rather, it focusses on households' attempts to maintain the service value of assets that are fixed (possibly temporarily).

In other words, fixities in household production functions create natural barriers to adjustment to economic change. In turn, these barriers often produce economic exigencies for the losers in situations of dynamic economic change. Hemmed in by their own maximizing behaviour, economic agents naturally turn to the political process, seeking one or another form of government support. Faced with real economic exigency, losers, especially organized losers, place heavy pressure on government to respond in an ameliorative manner. The result is often policies that increase the artificial barriers to economic adjustment and growth.

HOUSEHOLD DECISION-MAKING BEHAVIOUR:
A THEORETICAL ANALYSIS

Basic to this hypothesis is the modern theory of household behaviour, advanced by theorists such as Becker (1965; 1975), in which the concept of a household production function replaces the traditional concept of a utility function. This emphasis on the household as a producing unit may surprise some readers since standard economic analysis has focussed on the firm as the basic decision-making unit where production is involved. Moreover, technological constraints on economic agents' ability to adjust to economic change are normally thought to operate at the level of the plant or the firm.

This view of the problem overlooks the fact that many of the firm's variable inputs involve human labour, which wears two economic hats so far as production is concerned. First, human labour is an input into the production process, generating output. Second, human beings produce utility by combining goods and time into utility-giving services and activities (see Michael and Becker 1973).

In the traditional theory of consumer choice, the consuming unit maximizes its utility from the consumption of various goods and services purchased in the marketplace, subject to an income or wealth constraint. In this framework, the household is viewed simply as a consumer of goods and services.

Becker, like most modern theorists, takes a different tack, emphasizing not only the household's command over goods, which it gains primarily through its labour services, but also the way in which it uses and allocates its time. Time is valuable not only because it is in limited supply but because it is usually combined with other goods and services to produce objects or entities of enjoyment (utility). In brief, this approach envisions the primary objects of consumer choice as the various commodities that the household can produce by combining time with goods and services purchased in the market. In other words, purchased goods and services and time are *inputs* into a household production function from which flow final, utility-giving commodities.[4] The constraints to maximizing utility are the constraints of the production function as well as those of the household's time and income.

FIXITIES IN THE HOUSEHOLD PRODUCTION FUNCTION

With its treatment of purchased goods and time as inputs into a production process, the modern theory of the household has a foundation comparable to that of the theory of the firm. The question arises, therefore, whether one can distinguish among these inputs in a manner analogous to the way in which the Marshallian theory of the firm distinguishes between inputs that are variable and those that are fixed in the short run.

In my view, one can construct a convincing analogy between the fixed-variable distinction of traditional production theory and the household production function, using household assets' characteristics of portability/transferability or lack thereof. First, note that many of the inputs into the household production function are assets, such as automobiles, houses, and household equipment, that make up an important part of the household's nonhuman capital or wealth. In addition, command over all the purchased inputs into the household's production function depends in large part on its earning power and, therefore, on its human capital. Thus, the household's wealth – human and nonhuman, pecuniary and nonpecuniary – enters its production function directly or indirectly.

Now, all assets can be characterized in terms of their potential portability and transferability. Moreover, there is a natural parallel between the variable-fixed cost distinction and the degree of portability/transferability of assets. Implicitly at least, the assets in the household production function can be described in terms of their variability or fixity.

Let us proceed more deliberately. A household's wealth, W^H, comprises its human capital, HC, and its nonhuman capital, NHC. The former can be divided into skill, S, experience, E, and seniority/tenure, T. The latter can be divided into physical assets, A, money, M, and nonmonetary financial assets, F. Thus:

$$W^H = \text{NHC} + \text{HC}.$$
$$\text{NHC} = A + M + F.$$
$$\text{HC} = S + E + T.$$
$$W^H = A + M + F + S + T + E.$$

Clearly, the less portable and transferable one of these components, the more difficulty for an economic agent who seeks to adjust to change by moving it or selling it. Thus, the rapidity with which a household can adjust to economic change depends on the *composition* of its wealth. If it is primarily in physical assets or if it is composed of a highly specialized form of human capital, the household's ability to adjust to economic change *may* be (but is not necessarily) quite limited. To the extent that a household's assets are neither portable nor easily transferable, adjustment in the form of a geographic (or occupational) move may entail heavy capital losses.[5] If it does, the utility-maximizing household has good reason to resist adjusting, hoping that economic conditions will again reverse themselves or that a better deal can be made by waiting.

Thus, just as the profit-maximizing firm minimizes losses in the short run by continuing to produce so long as revenue covers variable costs, the household *may* have strong economic reasons to remain in a given location following a plant closure, even though the area offers little prospect of remunerative employment in the foreseeable future and even though jobs are going begging elsewhere. Like the firm that continues to produce in the face of fixed costs that are too high to permit a profit, the household with fixed assets 'hangs in'.

A simple taxonomy may help make the point. Table 3 lists a number of types of household assets, distinguishing those that are portable from those that are more or less nonportable and those that are transferable from those that are more or less nontransferable, at least in the short term.

The matrix makes it clear that many household production functions involve fixities that may make it costly to adjust quickly to economic change. The largest portion of a typical household's nonhuman wealth comprises a house and an employer pension plan. Neither is portable, the pension is nontransferable, and under certain conditions, not infrequent when a plant closes, the house may be difficult to sell without a large capital loss. The household's other large asset is likely to be human capital, which is nontransferable and, if seniority and tenure rights are involved, may be nonportable as well. A spouse's labour-market attachment may also be nonportable.[6] Faced with a loss of these assets by making a move, the household may well react in a manner similar to that of the firm with fixed costs that are high and variable costs that are low.[7] It stays put, continuing to produce services so long as it can stave off bankruptcy.[8]

An example
Farming and farmers provide an excellent example of the ideas presented here, partly because a farmer's firm and household are often identical,

TABLE 3
A taxonomy of household assets

	Easily transferable	Nontransferable (or transferable with difficulty and/or loss)
Highly portable	Most commodities Financial assets	Human capital
Nonportable (or portable with difficulty and loss)	Owned home in most locales	Employer pension plan contributions Seniority rights or tenure Owned home in a declining single-industry town Spouse's job Local amenities or environment Local reputation Language?

making it easy to envision how fixities may influence household behaviour.

Most farm assets are location-specific, and the typical farm has a high ratio of fixed to variable costs.[9] (This fact accounts for the observed stability of farm production over the business cycle, with output being maintained even when commodity prices are quite depressed.) But fixities in farm production are not the only reason farmers may be slow to exit from farming. Since a change of industry is likely to require a change of location, farmers consider the impact of exit on the value of all their location-specific and individual-specific assets. Among these are not only their land, farm buildings, and equipment, which may be difficult to sell, but also local reputation and status, which are likely to be of particular importance in small, long-established communities. As Olson puts it, 'Most people who have lived any length of time in a community ... must have built up a considerable "capital value" in status and reputation, and the capital value is lost if they move to another community' (1964, 986).[10] The nontransferability and limited portability of local reputation and status help to explain the wide divergence of factor returns in agriculture; equalizing them by means of mobility would be nonoptimal since doing so would mean ignoring the capital losses of intercommunity mobility.

HOUSEHOLD FIXITIES AND INDUSTRIAL ADJUSTMENT

We can now begin to understand why even firms and industries that are labour-intensive, have a high ratio of variable to fixed costs, and have physical capital composed primarily of portable machinery and equipment may pose problems of economic adjustment and thereby command political support for industrial assistance of some sort. The classic example is the clothing and textiles firm, which is often located in a town that relies on one or a very few employers. It is not necessarily the firm that finds adjustment so difficult, but rather the households that have been supplying its labour services. Their production functions may be capital-intensive, even if that of the firm is not.

Perhaps, then, the growing concern with industrial adjustment and assistance is at least partly related to the changing nature of the household's wealth portfolio. The dramatic rise in the incidence of home ownership, the spread of employer pension plans, and the increasing importance of investment in human capital have increased the likelihood that economic change will generate capital losses for a household. The probability of capital losses is directly related to the degree to which a household's human capital has limited adaptability because it is either highly specialized or untrainable, to the degree to which seniority and tenure are establishment- and location-specific, and to the degree to which the household's nonhuman capital is in a form of assets that is neither portable nor easily transferable – in brief, to the proportion of fixities among the household's human and nonhuman assets.

5
Fixities in
government production functions

The inclusion of the household production function is an essential step in the analysis of economic adjustment. Nevertheless, it is only a step. In a fundamental sense, the analysis remains factually and logically incomplete. To close the politico-economic system with which we are grappling, we must consider a third economic agent – government. Of particular concern are the utility and hence the production functions of the two junior levels of government, the provincial and the municipal or local.

DEBT AND THE GOVERNMENT PRODUCTION FUNCTION

Just as we can speak of a firm's and a household's production function, we can refer to a government's production function. Governments, like firms and households, use capital and labour inputs to produce goods and services. Some of the services, particularly those provided at the local level, are produced using large amounts of capital relative to labour and usually call for substantial borrowing on the part of the government. The obligation to service the debt is location-specific: it falls on the shoulders of residents of the borrowing jurisdiction.

During the last fifty years, all levels of government have grown, absolutely and relatively.[1] The junior levels in particular have rapidly increased production in the form of municipal services (water, sewage, roads, and so on) and the provision of education and health services, all of which involve heavy capital expenditures.

The important factors here are not only the services themselves but also the increase in capital expenditures and the associated outstanding indebtedness.[2] The larger a government's capital stock and indebtedness, the more industrial decline and consequent population loss put financial pressure on those who remain behind. The difficulty is threefold:

– Per-capita government debt rises as population declines.
– The per-unit cost increases for public services that have large fixed-cost elements because of their capital intensity.
– Per-capita revenue falls because the population decline induces a reduction in equalization payments.

Thus, a net loss of population through out-migration, whatever its cause, can have important financial consequences for municipal and provincial governments.[3]

Migration-induced financial problems are, of course, greatest at the local level of government since households may leave the municipality without necessarily leaving the province, much less the nation. Moreover, a local government is likely to have a larger proportion of its tax base committed to paying for capital equipment and structures than do higher levels of government.[4]

GOVERNMENT DEBT: DATA AND IMPLICATIONS

It is well known that Canadians carry a heavy burden of government debt at the municipal as well as the federal and provincial levels. Table 4 shows that in Canada at the end of 1978 *local* governments' total direct debt per capita was nearly $1000. Nationwide averages, however, hide differences among provinces, and these, of course, cloak differences between munici-

TABLE 4
Local government debt in Canada, 1978

	Long-term debt (000,000s)	Total debt[a] (000,000s)	Population[b] (000s)	Long-term debt per capita	Total debt per capita
Newfoundland	$ 203.6	$ 256.5	570	$ 357	$ 450
Prince Edward Island	40.5	45.8	122	332	375
Nova Scotia	328.6	582.5	842	390	692
New Brunswick	230.7	298.3	695	332	429
Quebec	6,488.9	8,609.9	6,287	1,032	1,369
Ontario	4,922.3	5,351.2	8,450	583	633
Manitoba	616.9	745.7	1,033	597	722
Saskatchewan	281.4	354.9	948	297	374
Alberta	2,271.0	2,925.1	1,955	1,162	1,496
British Columbia	2,395.2	2,744.4	2,533	945	1,083
Total[c]	17,803.6	21,956.9	23,499	758	934

[a] Long-term debt, short-term borrowings, and other liabilities, minus sinking fund.
[b] As of July 1978.
[c] Includes small amounts for Yukon and the Northwest Territories.

SOURCE: Canada (1981a), tables 15, 18.

palities – a point of some importance to the subject of this study. Provincially, the per-capita amounts ranged from a low of $374 in Saskatchewan to a high of $1496 in Alberta. Interestingly, the Atlantic provinces had lower per-capita averages than did most of the central or western provinces. However, the East's relatively small population bases make those provinces more vulnerable to the effects of out-migration. A loss of 50,000 persons (about 13,000 families) would have raised the per-capita debt by $33 in New Brunswick but only $4 in Ontario. The same arithmetic can have spectacular results at the local level. If a sizeable number of people leave a relatively small municipality, those who remain behind may have to carry a dramatic increase in per-capita debt.

It would seem, then, that different levels of government are likely to view economic adjustment through different sets of glasses. At least some local governments may be less than enthusiastic about federal policies that support high mobility of economic resources, especially the geographic mobility of labour. Migration may be economically optimal from a national standpoint but not from a regional or local one.[5] Given Canada's small population rather thinly spread over a huge expanse of land, any substantial change in economic geography can have important effects on the economic well-being, financial stability, and viability of at least some local governments.[6]

CONCLUSION

In sum, admitting government production functions into the theoretical analysis reveals even more complications in the issue of economic adjustment. We have already seen that inclusion of the household production function suggests that households may have good economic reasons for being unwilling to move even if the firms for which their members previously worked find it relatively easy to adjust geographically. The further addition of government as a separate economic agent (perhaps, at the local level, representing those who remain behind) suggests that powerful political forces may oppose economic adjustment by out-migration, even if the job losers, the people directly involved, are willing to migrate. That is, even if firms and households find adjustment relatively easy, fixities in government production functions may create political resistance to relocation policies on the part of those who stay behind.

To put the issue in terms more specific to welfare theory, adjustment assistance may require more than a subsidy to workers who migrate. It may also require a compensating subsidy to those left behind, offsetting the higher per-capita costs of maintaining local facilities and public goods whose costs are more or less fixed.

6
Household wealth:
its growth and composition

The hypothesis that fixities in household and government production functions help to shape government policies relating to economic adjustment is interesting, but we have not yet tested it. The next three chapters are an attempt to do so.

For this empirical analysis, it is useful to realize that the fixities hypothesis is really composed of three subsidiary ones:

– That the importance of fixities has grown in recent years.
– That the existence of fixities influences economic behaviour, in particular decisions to migrate.
– That the existence of fixities influences political behaviour, in particular the willingness of governments to supply a measure of aid or protection by means of industry- or firm-related policies.

In other words, that fixities exist is an idea rooted in a particular approach to household behaviour and in the notion of the nontransferability and nonportability of some assets; hence I take it as given from now on. The relevance of the hypothesis, however, depends on assets with the requisite characteristics having a growing importance in household decisions. This subhypothesis is the subject of the next chapter. Evidence that fixities influence household behaviour is a necessary but not sufficient condition to establish a link with industrial policy. The ultimate test is whether that influence has affected government's industrial policies, a hypothesis that unfortunately is much easier to support by casual observation than by careful empirical testing, as we shall see in Chapter 8.

The readers should be warned that they will not find any rigorous tests here. Providing them is impossible for two reasons. First, the existing data bases on wealth are so scanty as to preclude econometric testing of either of the two behavioural hypotheses. Thus, in Chapters 7 and 8 I have relied on case studies, and one can rarely, if ever, find the sort that clinches an argument. At best, one must use several examples, as I have done here. Second, behavioural hypotheses ultimately concern the motives that underlie observed behaviour, and establishing motivation is notoriously difficult. For the behaviour of households and firms, we can obviate the problem by assuming the maximization of utility or profits. For government, however, one cannot test definitively on the basis of observed behaviour itself. So we, like most juries, must rely on circumstantial evidence.

CHANGES IN HOUSEHOLD WEALTH

During the last several decades, a fundamental change in capitalist economies has been a widespread increase in household wealth. This section presents evidence not only on the growth of that wealth but also on changes in its composition. From the standpoint of the fixities hypothesis, it is the composition that matters most.

Home ownership
The rise in Canadian families' wealth and the sources of that rise are shown in Tables 5 through 8. Notice that the tables, like the following discussions, define nonhuman wealth as the household's physical and financial assets minus its debt. They do not include data on private-pension-plan claims, which are discussed in a later section.

Table 5 shows that Canadian families at all income levels enjoyed a substantial rise in nonhuman wealth between 1959 and 1977, with most of the increase occurring during the 1970s. Since homes make up about 60 per cent of Canadian households' nonhuman wealth (see Table 6), much of the change seems attributable to changes in the market value of housing, which rose very rapidly during the inflationary 1970s (presumably aided by the coming of age, marriage, and settling down of the baby-boom generation). The increase in home equity took place at all income levels (see Table 7) and had the effect of reducing wealth differentials among the various income groups.[1]

Home ownership not only accounts for a large proportion of the value of household assets[2]; it is also widespread. More than half of all Canadian families are homeowners, and that percentage has varied little since 1956 (see Table 7). Not surprisingly, ownership is highest among the upper income groups, but it is substantial even among Canadians with very low current incomes. Only in the last decade have fewer than 40 per cent of Canadian families with incomes of less than $5000 been homeowners. For those low-income families who are homeowners, the home represents a

TABLE 5
Average net worth of Canadian families (current dollars)

Income group	1959	1964	1970	1977
Less than $3,000	$ 4,071	$ 4,291	$ 7,040	$ 16,656
$ 3,000–4,999	5,479	5,586	10,192	23,338
$ 5,000–6,999	8,730	8,082	10,171	24,077
$ 7,000–9,999	10,324	10,862	12,731	31,001
$10,000–14,999			18,114	33,511
$15,000–24,999	{23,741}	{30,186}	33,876	47,198
$25,000 and more			94,940	117,495

NOTE: Net worth is defined as total assets minus total debt. The following items are included in the calculations for each year. Notice that claims on private pension funds are not included in any year.

	1959	1964	1970	1977
Assets				
Cash on hand			x	x
Bank deposits	x	x	x	x
Other savings deposits	x	x	x	x
Canada Savings Bonds	x	x	x	x
Other bonds	x	x	x	x
Publicly traded stocks		x	x	x
Shares in investment clubs		x	x	x
Other financial assets	x	x	x	x
Market value of home	x	x	x	x
Vacation home and automobile			x	x
Other real estate		x	x	x
Debt				
Charge accounts	x	x	x	x
Instalment debt	x	x	x	x
Secured bank loans	x	x	x	x
Other-collateral bank loans	x	x	x	x
Home-improvement loans	x	x	x	x
Other bank loans	x	x	x	x
Loans from consumer loan companies, credit unions, and caisses populaires	x	x	x	x
Other institutional loans	x	?	x	x
Miscellaneous debts and loans	x	?	x	x
Mortgage debt on home and vacation home	x	?	x	x

SOURCES: For 1959: Canada (1958); for 1964: Canada (1966, table 63); for 1970: Canada (1973, table 73); for 1977: Canada (1980, table 33).

TABLE 6
Percentage distribution of household assets

	1964	1970	1977
Liquid assets	18.2%	18.1%	16.4%
Other financial assets[a]	9.5	9.7	6.9
Market value of home	59.7	57.2	60.7
Other fixed assets[b]	12.6	15.0	16.0
Total	100.0	100.0	100.0

[a] Excludes RRSPs and other pension plan wealth.
[b] Investment in other real estate, vacation homes, automobiles.

SOURCES: For 1964: Canada (1966, table 31); for 1970: Canada (1973, table 51); for 1977: Canada (1980, table 22).

TABLE 7
Home ownership and average home equity

	1956	1959	1964	1970	1977
Income group					
Less than $3,000	–	$ 6,128[a]	$ 6,125[a]	$10,924	$26,911
$ 3,000–4,999	–	8,641[a]	7,665[a]	12,560[a]	30,341
$ 5,000–6,999	–	9,789	8,841	12,385	26,729
$ 7,000–9,999	–	11,555	9,834	13,995	33,146
$10,000–14,999	–			15,768	28,704
$15,000–24,999	–	19,079	14,174	20,224	30,882[a]
$25,000–34,999	–			34,645	39,267
$35,000 and more	–				59,250
Overall average equity	$ 5,456	$ 9,250	$ 8,801	$14,556	$33,968
Average mortgage	$ 2,318	$ 2,416	$ 3,358	$ 4,080	$ 9,875
Percentage of homeowners					
All families	54.6%	55.6%	54.2%	53.8%	59.6%
Families with incomes ≤ $5,000	–	48.6%[a]	43.4%[a]	45.6%[a]	35.7%[a]
Families with incomes ≥ $10,000	–	83.7%	77.0%	72.7%[a]	75.0%[a]

[a] Unweighted average

SOURCES: For 1956: Canada (1955); for 1959: Canada (1958, 22, and table 45); for 1964: Canada (1966, table 60); for 1970: Canada (1973, table 40); for 1977: Canada (1980, table IV-14).

TABLE 8
Average net worth of homeowners and nonhomeowners

Income group	1970		1977	
	Homeowners	Nonhomeowners	Homeowners	Nonhomeowners
Less than $3,000	$15,028	$ 1,316	$ 47,278	$ 2,182
$ 3,000–4,999	20,213	1,935	52,395	4,592
$ 5,000–6,999	18,580	2,599	49,265	4,606
$ 7,000–9,999	19,666	3,392	61,676	6,219
$10,000–14,999	24,653	4,985	55,891	7,864
$15,000–24,999	{48,876}	{27,445}	55,032	11,814
$25,000 and more			128,277	45,711

SOURCES: For 1970: Canada (1973, tables 16 and 56); for 1977: Canada (1980, table 33).

very substantial amount of wealth (see Table 8). In fact, for most low- and middle-income households, to be without equity in a home is to be largely without wealth. As Table 8 shows, the net worth of homeowners is many times higher than that of nonhomeowners who have the same income. In 1977, the ratio of homeowners' net worth to nonhomeowners' varied from 22 in the lowest income level to 3 at the highest.[3] Moreover, those differences increased especially at the lower income levels; between 1970 and 1977 the ratio for the lowest group doubled from 11 to 22.

The statistics on household wealth suggest:

– Canadian families at all income levels have more to lose (or gain) from unexpected changes in asset values than they did two decades ago.
– Public policies that focus solely or primarily on current income levels may be seriously out of tune with the concerns of households as wealth holders. In fact, the income statistics are seriously misleading in that they fail to capture the imputed income from the major source of household wealth: the home.
– By the same token, the wealth statistics mislead to the extent that changes in the market value of housing caused by changing local conditions primarily affect paper wealth and do not reflect changes in the real flow of imputed housing services that the homeowner receives.

The location of owned homes
Clearly, home ownership has played an important role in increasing the levels of household wealth in the past two decades. In and of itself, however, home ownership is not a particularly significant factor in determining geographic mobility – if the dwelling is easily saleable (that is, if a

sale will not entail a large capital loss). But if the local real estate market is thin or weak, the fixity problem arises.

Is this situation likely? An examination of data on the location of home ownership is suggestive. Table 9 shows that home ownership is greatest in the Atlantic region – the part of Canada that has suffered economic decline longest and most severely. Moreover, the percentage of homeowners with no mortgage debt is highest there. This fact is significant not only because it suggests that home equity is a relatively large proportion of wealth and hence relatively important for residents of the Atlantic region,[4] but also because it implies that most homeowners there must bear the full brunt of a total loss of market value (at least an unexpected loss[5]), rather than sharing it with mortgage holders.

TABLE 9
Home ownership by region, 1977

	Atlantic provinces	Quebec	Ontario	Prairie provinces	BC	Total
Homeowners as percentage of all families	70.3	49.6	62.4	62.9	60.4	59.6
Percentage of homeowners with no mortgage debt	62.7	38.0	43.9	50.9	46.2	46.0
Equity in home as percentage of net worth	53.9	42.4	47.6	35.7	42.9	43.7
Average mortgage ($)	5,206	8,364	11,905	8,373	12,201	9,875

SOURCES: Canada (1979b) and Canada (1980).

TABLE 10
Home ownership by size of area of residence, 1977

	Population of area of residence					
	500,000+	100,000–499,000	30,000–99,999	15,000–29,999	Small urban area	Rural area
Homeowners as percentage of all families	49.0	57.4	54.4	60.5	67.3	80.4
Percentage of homeowners without mortgage	35.7	35.0	43.4	48.9	60.2	62.4
Average equity ($)		39,377			26,180	

SOURCES: See sources for Table 9.

Table 10 pinpoints somewhat better the importance of home ownership in places where the housing market is likely to be either thin or particularly sensitive to plant shutdowns. The smaller the population centre, the more the market value of housing is likely to depend on the economic health of a single industry, firm, or plant. And the data show that both home ownership overall and ownership without a mortgage are highest in the smaller communities – the ones most vulnerable to industrial decline.

Of course, not all small communities are dependent on a single industry, but many are. Table 11 presents data on single-sector communities, defined as those in which one resource or activity absorbs at least 30 per cent of local employment. It shows there are a large number of single-sector communities in Canada, a fact highly relevant to the fixities hypothesis and so potentially a factor in the demand for industrial policies. It is also worth noting that, in 1976, of the thirty-three single-sector communities whose principal economic activity was manufacturing, twenty-five were in Quebec and thirteen of these were in the heavily protected textile, clothing, or shoe industries.

TABLE 11
Single-sector communities by region and industrial sector, 1976

Industrial sector	Atlantic provinces	Quebec	Ontario	Prairie provinces	BC, Yukon, & NWT	Total
Manufacturing (textiles, clothing, knitting, leather)	1	13	2	0	0	16
Manufacturing (other)	0	12	4	1	0	17
Mining	10	14	16	14	18	72
Wood based[a]	20	46	22	4	28	120
Food processing	2	3	5	3	0	13
Fishing	47	1	1	0	0	49
Public administration[b]	6	8	6	4	3	27
Other[c]	5	4	4	5	3	21
Prairie service centres	0	0	0	91	0	91
Total	91	101	60	122	52	426

NOTES: A single-sector community is a centre that depends upon one resource or one type of activity. It is defined as having at least 30 per cent of its employment in one sector, which may comprise a number of different but related SIC groups.

[a] Includes pulp and paper mills.
[b] Includes health and education.
[c] Includes transportation and tourism.
SOURCE: Canada (1979a, 55-6 and 80-1).

TABLE 12
Growth of the private pension plans, 1960–80

Size of group	1960		1976		1980	
	Plans	Members	Plans	Members	Plans	Members
5	a	a	4,463	9,952	3,170	7,233
5-14	5,037	24,000	4,327	37,052	3,851	33,500
15-99	2,613	101,000	4,542	174,472	4,853	190,596
100-499	892	193,000	1,587	350,416	1,886	413,060
500-1999	249	249,000	471	455,571	549	534,775
2000+	129	1,248,000	235	2,875,035	277	3,296,265
Total	8,920	1,815,000	15,625	3,902,498	14,586	4,475,429
Members as a percentage of labour force		28.3		37.9		38.8
Members as a percentage of labour force 25 years old and over		36.2		51.9		53.0

a Data not available.

SOURCE: Canada (1982b, 14).

Private pension plans
Another common household asset whose importance has increased dramatically in recent decades is the private pension plan. Table 12 shows the growth of the private pension system in Canada since 1960. The absolute number of persons covered increased by almost 250 per cent in two decades, and the proportion of the labour force covered rose markedly. The increase in coverage was even more marked for labour force participants twenty-five years of age and more, an important consideration for the fixities hypothesis since young workers are less likely than their elders to care about pension-plan coverage.

The statistics, of course, leave unanswered the questions of 1) how portable private pension plans are; 2) whether their degree of nonportability has changed in recent decades; and 3) how much impact their portability (or the lack of it) has on employee mobility. These issues are taken up in the next chapter.

Seniority and tenure
Clearly, seniority and tenure may be fixities, but their growth is difficult to quantify. Not only is there a lack of data, but in the case of seniority it is not clear what the appropriate units would be for making intertemporal or geographic comparisons. Suffice it to say that the growth of union mem-

bership in the 1960s and 1970s undoubtedly increased the number of workers covered by explicit seniority provisions, although many may already have been 'covered' by implicit contractual arrangements. The increase in the percentage of professional workers, particularly their growing numbers in the public and quasi-public sectors, suggests that the number of workers covered by contractual tenure arrangements has also grown substantially during the past two decades.

SUMMARY

In sum, household wealth has increased substantially and at all nominal income levels over the past few decades. This wealth takes many forms. It is particularly reflected in widespread home ownership and participation in pension plans, in increased investments in individual skills and training, in the quasi-property rights to jobs conveyed by explicit seniority provisions and tenure, and in the increased value placed on local amenities and environment by an increasingly leisure-consuming and health-conscious public.

Earlier chapters argued that much of this wealth has the fixity characteristics of nonportability and/or nontransferability (the reader may find the argument more convincing after reading some of the case studies in the next chapter). This chapter has shown that home ownership has grown and that there are many single-sector, or industrially thin, communities where home ownership is especially likely to have fixity characteristics. Pension plans have certainly increased, and so have seniority and job tenure. Ways in which these kinds of wealth may have influenced mobility decisions and industrial policy are the subjects of the next two chapters.

7
The behavioural response to fixities in household production functions: some case studies

The next step in testing the fixities hypothesis is to determine whether fixities, potential or actual, in household production functions have influenced household behaviour. The evidence comprises five short studies. The first two relate to housing, although each also touches on other factors: the provision of local-government services in one case; various impediments to mobility, such as seniority, in the others. The third study also relates to a variety of potential fixities, with emphasis on attachment to a specific locale. The fourth examines the impact on interprovincial migration of provincial differences in the maximum weeks of eligibility for Unemployment Insurance benefits, and the last considers vesting provisions in private pension plans.

MODERN NORTHERN COMMUNITIES

One way in which to illustrate the role of potential fixities in household and government production functions is to examine the development of northern mining communities that companies have built up since the Second World War. In many older settlements that were or have become single-sector mining or manufacturing communities, the dominant employer took little or no responsibility for the development and upkeep of housing, the infrastructure, and other community facilities. (In fact, during the late nineteenth century, some eastern Canadian towns lured firms with local subsidies and tax concessions [see Naylor 1975].) In contrast, the large companies that today undertake the development of communities in areas far from any major established settlement have had to take on the responsibility of building and maintaining facilities to serve and house the community. Moreover, if the industry declines or the ore runs out, the employer is under a good deal of pressure to compensate owners of homes and businesses, who face heavy capital losses. In effect, what would otherwise be fixities in household and government production functions are shifted partially or totally to the firm.[1]

Uranium City
An interesting example of these shifts appears in the story of Uranium City, Saskatchewan, a town built by Eldorado Nuclear Ltd. for its workers in the north. In 1982, Eldorado announced that it would close its Uranium City mine, which means the death of a community of 3000 persons after thirty prosperous years. Although the company's decision apparently came as a shock to most of the town's residents, adjustment for most of them has been made much less difficult because jobs in other mining towns are relatively plentiful for experienced miners. Moreover, Eldorado Nuclear will bear most of the costs associated with property-value loss. Approximately half of the families in Uranium City owned their homes (the figure in 1971 was 43 per cent [1971 Census]), many of them bought from Eldorado, which is now presumably expected to write off any outstanding mortgage debt and loans for household furnishings. Moreover, a consultant's report stated that the 170 owners of noncompany homes and the owners of businesses should receive 'indemnification' up to a maximum of $58,000 for houses and $150,000 for businesses (*Globe and Mail*, 30 June 1982, p. 3).[2]

Schefferville and Labrador City
In November 1982, the Iron Ore Company (IOC) of Canada announced that it was permanently closing its aging iron-ore mines at Schefferville, Quebec, and Labrador City, Newfoundland. The closures effectively mean the death of two towns, which were originally built by the company.

In 1981, 25 per cent of Schefferville's 2000 people had lived there twenty years or more, while 30 per cent of Labrador City's 11,500 residents had lived there for ten to twenty years. About 30 per cent of the households in Schefferville and 70 per cent of those in Labrador City owned their homes (Bradbury 1982).[3] IOC had built most of both towns' housing stock for sale or rental. To stabilize the work force, it had encouraged home ownership by providing long-term (often thirty-year) mortgages that included a buy-back provision from first owners within the first five to ten years of the dwelling's lifespan.[4] Moreover, the mortgage rate in many cases was substantially below market rates. Since most immigrants to Schefferville and Labrador City did not expect to remain there longer than ten years, homeowners bore little or no risk of capital loss if the mines closed unexpectedly.

In the event, the company provided even more protection that it had guaranteed. During the two years before announcing closure, as dwindling demand resulted in a decline of the work force and emigration from Schefferville and Labrador City, IOC provided financial assistance to some families no longer covered by the buy-back provision who were attempting to sell their homes in a deeply depressed market (Bradbury 1982, 19). It is not clear whether IOC will extend similar arrangements to the remaining long-term homeowners now that it has officially announced the closure.

Transferring fixities

The experiences in Uranium City, Schefferville, and Labrador City indicate that the problem of fixities is a potentially real one for households. Because the risks of a dwindling ore body or market are substantial (Eldorado experienced both), mining families are loathe to make commitments, such as the purchase of a home, that could result in large capital losses if the mine shuts down. One way around the problem is for the mining company to shoulder all or a large part of the burden of risk. In the cases described, this transfer of risk appears to have taken place. By building the infrastructure and facilities and owning some of them, by being willing to buy back the homes it has sold to its employees, and by forgiving mortgages and loans for furniture and other household goods, the company absorbs risks and losses that households and local taxpayers would have had to bear. In other words, what might otherwise be fixities in household and local government production functions are made variable costs or eliminated altogether by their transfer to the firm's account.[5]

This transfer, of course, adds substantially to the mining companies' own fixed costs. One result is that today the development of new ore bodies does not always involve the creation of a community, even in the northern hinterland. An alternative, increasingly used as transportation technology has improved, is to have the work force 'commute' – perhaps for a week at a time – from some larger, more diversified community. For example, Eldorado staffs its new mine at Key Lake, Saskatchewan by having its workers commute from Saskatoon. An alternative is a government-created and government-financed regional centre in a mining area, such as the one at Leaf Rapids, Manitoba. In both cases, the mining companies are expected to take a full share of such a community's tax burden (Siemens 1973). By shouldering the cost of transporting their work force a distance of several hundred miles and/or by assuming part of the cost of a regional centre – costs that disappear once the mine is shut down – mining companies are translating what would otherwise be fixed costs into variable ones.[6]

If few new towns appear as Canada's northern resources are developed, part of the reason will be an attempt to avoid the fixities (costs) that the firm or its employees would have to bear if full-fledged communities were built around ore bodies with a limited life and in the face of uncertain market demand.

COUNCIL HOUSING IN GREAT BRITAIN

Studies involving Great Britain's council housing – public rental housing that is heavily subsidized – provide examples of how housing and housing policy can affect the willingness to move and reduce geographic mobility.[7] Further, they illustrate that home ownership is not a necessary condition of housing tenure's becoming a fixity in the household production function. Explicit and implicit subsidies, including rent control, also create fixities to the extent that the subsidies are nontransferable (that is, tenants cannot sell them for their capitalized value) and nonportable (that is, a mover cannot expect to obtain a subsidized or rent-controlled unit more or less immediately in a new location).[8]

Tenants rent council housing from a local government authority, which builds, owns, and allocates the units among prospective tenants.[9] Subsidies, which are substantial, come from both central and local taxes. They vary over time and space and sometimes with tenants' income. Nationwide, subsidies made up 40 per cent of local-housing-authority income in 1951, 33 per cent in 1961, and 26 per cent in 1967. Local differences are considerable; in 1966, for example, subsidies ranged from 14 per cent of local housing revenue in Oxford and Brighton to 70 per cent in Newcastle (Gray 1968, 28-32). These differentials reflect differences not only in income – many local housing authorities give rent rebates to low-income tenants – but in the construction costs and interest rates prevailing at the time the council houses were built.

Council housing is widespread in Great Britain. In 1971, it made up 31 per cent of all dwellings, a figure that had climbed from 13 per cent in 1947 and 26 per cent in 1960 (Murie, Niner, and Watson 1976, 4, 91). Owner-occupation is also on the rise, from 42 per cent of the housing stock in 1960 to 50 per cent in 1971. The concomitant fall in private rental housing (only 14 per cent of the stock in 1971) has meant that increasingly, a family that wants to rent accommodation – a good choice if one wants to reduce impediments to geographic mobility – must choose council housing. Moreover, since the council houses are, on average, much newer than those that are privately rented, they are more likely to contain various modern amenities. These phenomena plus the substantial subsidies for council housing mean that most local housing authorities have long waiting lists (Murie, Niner, and Watson 1976, 129-30).

Given the combination of subsidies and queues for council houses, it is not surprising to find considerable evidence that council-housing tenants are less likely to move than their counterparts in the occupant-owned and privately rented housing sectors and that a very high proportion of moves takes place within tenures (Murie, Niner, and Watson 1976, 39; Gray 1968, 41). Because council-housing tenants cannot take their subsidy with them (unless a swap can be arranged with a tenant of another housing authority), one would expect them to be reluctant to move to another locale, even if a better job awaits them there, unless its council housing has vacancies or unless they are placed high on a waiting list. Since the housing authorities establish priorities that often include length of residence in a borough (as well as such factors as age, family size, and 'housing need'), the chances that a person making an intercity move would be given a preferential position on a waiting list are remote indeed. Thus Gray (1968, 41) states, 'The conclusion that local authority allocation policies seriously inhibit household mobility seems strong, if not inescapable.'

The Hughes and McCormick study
The conclusion that council-housing policies inhibit intercity or interregional moves is reinforced by a careful empirical study by Hughes and McCormick (1981). They found that council-housing tenants are much less likely to migrate (defined as an interregional move) than owner-occupiers and other renters, even after taking into consideration other factors affecting mobility, such as education, age, unemployment, and occupation.[10] Hughes and McCormick attribute these lower rates of geographic mobility to council-housing administrative policies that discourage long-distance migration. They find, however, that council-housing tenure does not appear to inhibit local moves, presumably because local residents are preferred to immigrants in council-housing queues.

The Hartlepool study
Some more evidence on the way in which council-housing subsidies and policies influence job mobility comes from an in-depth study of the mobility of employees who worked at British Steel Corporation's (BSC) Hartlepool works (Smith 1978). In 1978, BSC closed its antiquated steel-making plant at Hartlepool, with a loss of more than 1100 jobs. Some employment opportunities existed at BSC's plants in nearby South Teesside and in other parts of the UK. The study found that the affected workers had only a limited willingness to move although there were very few job

openings in Hartlepool, which already had a 10 per cent unemployment rate. A variety of factors contributed to general immobility, including: 1) the limited demand in Britain for the redundant employees' skills (or lack of them); 2) the workers' perceptions of their job prospects, whether correct or not; 3) strong nonpecuniary preferences by many workers and their families for remaining in Hartlepool. Nevertheless, it is interesting to probe the issue further.

South Teesside, where BSC had some jobs available, is just across the river from Hartlepool, but poor road and bridge conditions and the lack of good, direct public transport make commuting there from Hartlepool very time-consuming (about an hour each way by car, much more by public transport). Nevertheless, although a third of the workers sampled said they were willing to work for BSC in South Teesside, only 12 per cent indicated a willingness to move their homes in order to take up that employment. One factor was strong local attachment, including family ties.[11] Another reason was that a substantial portion of the Hartlepool workers were council-housing tenants. Because of a long waiting list, it takes several years to obtain council housing in the area that serves South Teesside.[12] The alternative was home ownership; giving up subsidized housing in an area to which they were attached for owned housing that saddled them with large mortgages and heavy payments was an exchange few would want to make.

Interestingly, 25 per cent of the Hartlepool workers said they would be willing to work for BSC in other parts of the UK. (Thirty-three per cent were willing to move to take a non-BSC job.) Of the would-be movers to other BSC jobs, 51 per cent were owner-occupiers and 35 per cent were council-housing tenants. Among the latter, only two in ten perceived that it would be difficult to find suitable accommodation in another region, although this optimism was not warranted by the council-housing situation in other parts of England (Smith 1978, 68-9).[13]

Thus, it appears that the willingness of council-housing tenants to move is clearly related to their perception of the availability of council housing elsewhere.

Other considerations

The Hartlepool study also turned up some other phenomena that relate to mobility and support the fixities hypothesis. One factor reducing willingness to change jobs prior to closure of the Hartlepool works was the knowledge that employees made redundant by the closure would receive payments averaging £4207 per manual worker (about half was required by the Redundancy Act of 1965, the rest was mainly *ex gratia*). In addition, moving to the BSC works at South Teesside would mean a loss of seniority and a consequent cut in pay (at the same time that commuting or housing costs would rise). In fact, the seniority rule, whereby a new entrant to a works, regardless of his experience at other plants, must start at the bottom of the promotion ladder, was found to be a major problem in inducing workers to switch from one BSC works to another, either before or after closure of the Hartlepool plant.

Some other factors influencing the Hartlepool workers' mobility were their spouses' jobs, the attachment of their children to particular schools, and the fact that housing prices are lower in the northeast of England than in most other areas of the country.

Moving costs *per se*, however, were an unimportant factor in the mobility decisions of the Hartlepool workers. Thus, the study implies that financial incentives have only a limited ability to promote geographic mobility if the existence of fixities means a move would produce large wealth losses.

Overall, what the Hartlepool study seems to indicate is that it is the wealth lost by moving because of the existence of fixities, rather than the out-of-pocket costs associated with a move, that dominates mobility decisions.[14]

THE MACK TRUCK PLANT CLOSURE

It is interesting to compare the findings from the Hartlepool study with those of Dorsey's study (1967) of workers' response to the Mack Truck Company's announcement, in 1961, that it would close its antiquated plant in Plainfield, New Jersey and move its operations to a newly constructed facility in Hagerstown, Maryland. The affected workers had the choice of transferring to the new plant or remaining at the New Jersey one until it actually closed, when they were eligible to receive substantial severance payments.

Of the 2700 workers, only about 250 made the interplant transfer. In a survey of both groups, Dorsey found that moving costs did not figure importantly in the mobility decision. The workers who remained behind were motivated by a number of factors, among them the expectation of substantially lower wages at the Hagerstown plant[15] and the availability of generous severance payments bolstered by Unemployment Insurance benefits for those who became unemployed when the Plainfield plant closed. Of particular interest to the present study are the other factors that, according to Dorsey, played an important role in many workers' decisions not to move.

The choice between transferring and not transferring depended in good part on whether a worker's job-attachment was greater or less than his attachment to his area of residence. Not surprisingly, workers with seniority, a measure of job attachment and a fixity in our lexicon, had higher transfer rates. (Mack indicated, however, that seniority would be determined at the new plant.) Nevertheless, most workers were more attached to their New Jersey homes, with the strength of the attachment conditioned by the length of time they had lived in the area, children in school, family ties, and home ownership. Although Dorsey does not provide any information on whether transfer would have entailed capital losses in the sale of homes,[16] his study does provide evidence that attachment to a specific geographic location, clearly a fixity in household production functions, plays an important part in mobility decisions. Although most of the workers who remained behind suffered a period of unemployment, which was lengthy in some cases, and almost all had to accept considerably lower wages than they had received at Mack, there is no evidence that they regretted not having made the transfer.

Job-specific skills
The Mack Truck study also gives insight into the role of job-specific skills as a fixity affecting occupational mobility. Dorsey found that after the Plainfield plant closed, the skilled and the unskilled workers had little difficulty finding new jobs. However, the semiskilled group, the largest of those seeking new jobs, had the greatest adjustment problem. The source of their difficulty was their unrealistic wage expectations in light of their highly job-specific skills. The semiskilled workers could command a high wage at Mack because they had 'mastered the technique of operating one machine rapidly and efficiently' (p. 229). Now that this highly specific skill was no longer required, their lack of versatility (for example, their inability to read blueprints, use precision instruments, or operate a variety of machines) made them effectively unskilled, but they were unwilling to accept the low wage levels that that skill level commands.

REGIONAL VARIATIONS IN MAXIMUM PAYOUT PERIODS

An interesting example of a fixity created by a government program is supplied by Canada's Unemployment Insurance (UI) system. Under the UI plan that came into force in 1971, the maximum payout period for benefits varies directly with the regional or provincial unemployment rate as well as the national rate and the beneficiary's weeks of insured employment. The differentials are particularly marked for claimants who have only the minimum number of weeks of insured employment. For example, in the Maritimes, a region that usually has well-above-average unemployment rates, the maximum payout period for such workers ranges from forty to fifty weeks, about double the maximum in regions with below-average rates.[17]

This variation creates a fixity since eligibility to receive UI benefits is a nontransferable asset, and the maximum length of the payout period is not portable across regional boundaries. To the extent that this fixity influences household behaviour, one would predict that it would retard migration from regions with high unemployment (and a relatively long maximum payout period) to regions with low unemployment (and a relatively short maximum payout period). The impact should be greatest on low-income households since they are more likely to experience unemployment and UI benefits constitute a larger fraction of their earnings.

Those predictions are confirmed in Winer and Gauthier's study (1982) of fiscally induced migration in Canada. Among the variables they use to capture interprovincial differences in fiscal structure is one measuring the maximum period for which an unemployed person with the minimum amount of qualifying employment could draw benefits.[18] The results of their multiple regression analysis provide strong statistical support for the view that interprovincial differences in UI generosity have a substantial influence on interprovincial migration. Specifically, the coefficient on the UI variable in their estimating equations implies that generosity has substantially reduced the migration of low-income persons from the Maritimes to Ontario and the West, but not mobility within the Maritime provinces. For example, the results suggest that migration to Ontario was 35 to 42 per cent lower in 1977 than would have been the case in the absence of the 1971 changes to the UI system. And the positive coefficient on the UI variable for intra-Maritime moves suggests that the UI rules actually increased migration within the region.

These results are just what the fixities hypothesis predicts. A prospective migrant from the Maritimes to Ontario or the West foresees a 'capital loss' equal to the value of the forgone UI benefits times the likelihood that he or she will incur a spell of unemployment longer than the maximum number of weeks he or she would be eligible to receive UI benefits in the province of destination. For a person who is likely to be unemployed, such a loss would represent a substantial cost that must be weighed against the benefits from moving. If, however, the same person is considering moving to another part of the Maritimes, no such loss need be considered, although the probability of such a move's enhancing his or her employment and earnings prospects may be somewhat lower than in the case of a move to the West.

PENSION PLANS AND EMPLOYEE BEHAVIOUR

As we saw in Chapter 6, rights to private pension plans seem a likely factor in the fixities hypothesis. Their incidence has increased in recent decades; they are not transferable among individuals, and, except in cases of inter-governmental moves and a few multi-employer plans in the private sector, they are not portable either. But do these characteristics make pensions a fixity in household product functions? If so, is it one that has affected employee mobility? These are not rhetorical questions, for the issues here are more complex than they first appear.

Vesting
One reason for this complexity is that workers who leave jobs before their pension plan benefits are vested can generally get back their own contributions plus interest. Thus, although the plan may not be portable, the employee's contributions are – at least until the plan is vested. Even after vesting, some plans permit cash withdrawal on termination of employment (with forfeiture of the employer's contributions), and this is a popular choice, particularly among younger workers. For example, Rea and Pesando (1980) refer to a study of federal government workers who terminated that employment; in all age groups, the great majority chose cash withdrawal of their pension contributions and thereby forfeited claim to the government's. The subjects of that study, however, left their jobs before December 1957 when the minimum vesting requirement for government workers was five years' service. Moreover, cash withdrawal after vesting is no longer an option in many cases since changes in the legislation regulating private pension plans have often resulted in the 'locking-in' of both employee and employer contributions, preventing the worker whose pension benefits are vested from choosing current consumption over saving for retirement.[19]

As workers get older, the relative attractiveness of deferred benefits and present consumption naturally changes. Thus, the rules for the vesting of pension benefits become increasingly important to workers as their age rises. In Canada today, the minimum requirement for compulsory vesting of private pension plans is generally the '45 and 10' rule – that is, a terminating employee who is at least age 45 and has at least ten years of

TABLE 13
Vesting provisions of private pension plans, 1965-76

	Percentage of private-pension-plan members covered by rule	
Vesting rule	1965	1976
Immediate vesting	7	6
10 years or less of service or participation	30	54
11 to 19 years of service or participation	9	8
20 years or more of service or participation	15	4
45 years of age and 10 years of service	0	15
Other	17	13
No vesting	22	1
Total	100	100

SOURCE: Canada (1979c, vol. 1, table III-7, p. 45).

service with an employer when terminated is entitled to receive benefits from that employer's pension plan at the specified retirement age. Many plans have less stringent requirements than '45 and 10',[20] but most have some minimum (see Table 13). The important point here is that most vesting rules include years of service, and a terminating employee cannot carry credit for them from one employer to another. Thus, one would expect that a middle-aged or older worker whose length of service with an employer does not yet allow for vesting would be inhibited from changing employment.[21]

Thus, the theoretical impact of private-pension-plan nonportability on job mobility seems uncertain overall. For middle-aged and older workers, one would expect stringent vesting provisions to reduce mobility. The opposite may be true for younger workers if 'lock-in' regulations are involved; to a person with heavy current expenditure burdens, a high discount rate will make the value of a deferred pension twenty-five or thirty years in the future look small. A cash withdrawal can come in handy upon termination for these workers, and those who value it very highly may feel forced to change employment earlier than they had planned in order to prevent vesting and the consequent 'lock-in' of their contributions.

Benefits
Even after a pension plan is vested, a job change may affect its benefits. Most private plans pay out 'defined benefits' based on either career-average earnings or final years' average earnings. Especially in the latter case whether a retiree has worked for one or for several employers can

make a big difference. For example, assuming a 3 per cent inflation rate and a steep earnings profile, the expected benefit-to-contribution ratio for a worker with membership in four fully vested plans for nine years each is 1.6, but it is 2.7 for membership in one plan for thirty-six years (Canada 1979c, table 2, 7-10).[22] Thus, despite full vesting, job mobility can materially affect the return to each dollar of contribution.[23]

Empirical evidence
Although private pension plans contain provisions that might be expected, on average, to reduce job mobility, there is little or no hard evidence that they have been a major deterrent to mobility. Many workers, particularly those many years away from retirement, probably discount, ignore, or just do not make pension-plan calculations. For those who do tally up the net impact of job termination on pension plan benefits, other factors often, perhaps usually, dominate employment change decisions. Moreover, if anything, vesting provisions in private-sector pension plans have been liberalized during the past thirty years, making them less of a deterrent to job mobility.[24]

It is not surprising then that there is little or no hard evidence that private pension plans have affected job mobility. Rea and Pesando refer to US evidence that 'indicates that delayed vesting provisions may not have a major deterrent impact on labour mobility' (1980, 27-8). A Canadian study of the interaction of labour-mobility rates and vesting rules on pensionable service found that job mobility is high in Canada. Using simulation techniques, Prefontaine and Balcer constructed job-tenure curves for various age groups and used them to estimate the number of pensionable years of service under a '45 and 10' rule. The conclusion was:

Mobility rates in the labour force in Canada are such that the current regulatory policy of compulsory vesting at age 45 and 10 years of service will not produce any pension benefits for a large proportion of current workers. A further large segment will receive an inadequate level of pension income. (1979, 8-9)

The concern seems to be not that the pension system reduces job mobility, but that a high level of mobility undermines the pension benefits to which workers are entitled.[25]

In short, except for certain groups, it is hard to conclude that private pensions act as an important fixity in Canadian household production functions. To the extent that pensions are nonportable and nontransferable, they seem an obvious example of a fixity, but the situation is actually much more complicated. Part of the pension-plan contribution (the employee's own) is not 'fixed', and younger workers especially may value a partial but immediate lump-sum return more highly than later pension benefits. Thus, the behavioural consequences of pension plans seem to depend more on the worker's age and other factors than on the qualities they share with fixities.

CONCLUSION

The five case studies presented in this chapter suggest that the existence of household fixities may influence individual behaviour. This conclusion is particularly clear in the studies of the effects of housing, the Mack Truck closure, and the UI payout period. (The council housing and UI examples are especially interesting because the fixities do not involve ownership *per se* but assets that are government-created 'rights'.) In all three cases the available statistical evidence suggests that the fixities in various forms of household wealth substantially reduced geographic mobility.

The case study of the northern mining communities suggests that all parties involved – households, firms, and government – were well aware of the fixities problem. It has been dealt with by having the companies bear some of the risks of capital losses that would otherwise be borne by households, by socialization of the risks via lower wages and lower taxes, and most recently by a movement away from the community-building approach to northern mining development.

In contrast, there is little evidence that nonvested employer pension plans have had a dampening effect on interfirm or interindustry mobility in Canada. A possible conclusion is that one must be careful in assigning the term fixity and in applying the hypothesis. Other factors may bring about different behavioural results.

8
Fixities and
Canadian protectionist policies

Having seen that at least some kinds of fixities do influence household behaviour, we are now ready to test the link between them and government policies. Are interventionist industrial policies a response to the economic exigency that fixities may create for some individuals in times of economic adjustment? In an attempt to answer that question, this chapter looks for evidence that the existence of fixities has influenced tariff and import-quota policies. The first section examines recent changes in Canada's quota policies that affected the import of leather footwear but not of clothing. The second analyses the literature on the determinants of tariff protection and industrial assistance, focussing on Canadian studies but referring to work from the United States and Australia as well.

LEATHER FOOTWEAR AND CLOTHING IMPORT QUOTAS

An examination of recent decisions on shoe and clothing import quotas provides some support for the hypothesis that household fixities have influenced industrial policy. The analysis also illustrates some of the problems of testing the hypothesis.

In November 1981, the Canadian government lifted import quotas on leather footwear while leaving intact those on the clothing and, by extension, the textile industries. Eight months later, it reimposed limits on the import of shoes. Canadian shoe, clothing, and textile manufacturing are all industries that, in the absence of protective measures, face particularly stiff foreign competition.[1] The following analysis assumes that quotas in any of these areas prevent job loss and that their elimination causes it.

The lifting of the quotas
Let us start our analysis of the lifting of the quotas with a syllogism: 1) if the existence of fixities in household production functions is an implicit factor

in decisions to keep or lift quotas, and 2) if the fixities problem is most acute in industrially thin communities, one would predict that quotas would be more likely to be lifted (and less likely to be imposed in the first place) for an industry whose firms are concentrated in large urban centres. Almost by definition, the fixities problem is more acute in industrially thin communities since finding new employment after plant shutdowns there is more likely to require a geographic move than it is in an urban area. Moreover, as Table 10 showed, home ownership and the ratio of equity to mortgage debt are both higher in smaller communities than in large urban areas. Thus it appears safe to accept the second premise, and the decision to lift the import quotas on shoes seems to provide an opportunity to make at least a crude test of the fixities hypothesis.

Does the locational distribution of plants in the shoe and clothing/textile industries differ with respect to city size? Statistical information says it does, supporting the prediction that shoe manufacturers are much more likely to operate in large cities than are clothing/textile firms. In November 1981, when Ottawa made the decision to drop the quotas on shoes, a reported 21,000 workers were employed in the domestic footwear industry; within two months it had dropped to 13,000 persons. Seventy per cent of the employment was concentrated in four cities: Montreal, Quebec, Toronto, and Kitchener (*Montreal Gazette*, 16 January 1982, p. 61). Thus, one could argue that the industry's urban concentration made easier the decision to lift the quotas.

In contrast, the Canadian clothing and textile industries are much more dispersed, with many mills and plants located outside the larger cities (see Table 14).[2] Significantly, although the clothing and textile industries are centred in Quebec and to a lesser extent in Ontario, the most urbanized of the provinces, substantially more than a third of all the plants are scattered outside the major urban areas.

TABLE 14
Textile (and some clothing) mills in smaller communities, 1977

	Atlantic provinces	Quebec	Ontario	Western provinces	Total
Total mills and plants	16	439	254	31	740
Number in smaller communities	14	161	92	10	277
Percentage in smaller communities	87.5	36.7	36.2	32.2	37.4

SOURCE: Canadian Textile Journal (1977, 171-5).

TABLE 15
Single-sector communities: clothing and textiles, leather

	Industry	Product (SIC classification)
Clothing and textiles		
Quebec		
Acton Vale	Textile	Carpets, mats, and rugs
Cookshire	Clothing	Plastic items
Cowansville	Clothing	Plastic items
Farnham	Miscellaneous	Buttons, buckles, and fasteners
Huntingdon	Textile	Wool yarn and cloth
Louiseville	Clothing	Women's clothing
Magog	Clothing	Cotton yarn and cloth
Ormstown	Textile	Miscellaneous textiles
St-Cesaire	Clothing	Women's clothing
St-Honoré	Clothing	
St-Victor	Textile	Wool yarn and cloth
Ontario		
Iroquois	Textile	Miscellaneous textiles
Lanark	Clothing	Knitted items
Leather		
Quebec		
Richmond	Leather	Shoes
St-Tite	Leather	Shoes

NOTE: A single-sector community is defined as one in which 30 per cent of the total employed population is engaged in a single type of activity.

SOURCE: Canada (1979a, 62-78).

Significantly, too, data from 1976 show many more textile and clothing plants than shoe factories located in single-sector communities (see Table 15), where plant shutdowns often mean wholesale community disruption as displaced workers search for new jobs. The relative importance of clothing and textiles among single-sector communities could well have been an important factor in the government's deciding to implement and keep import quotas on clothing.

Thus, the data in Tables 14 and 15 are consistent with our hypothesis. Yet they are surely not definitive. The existence of fixities may have nothing to do with the policy decisions in November 1981. Keeping the import quotas on clothing while lifting those on shoes was also consistent with at least three other objectives: 1) supporting less-developed regions, such as eastern Quebec, where many clothing and textile firms happen to be located; 2) aiding industries that employ large numbers of workers

(Canadian clothing and textile firms employ more than eight times as many workers as do shoe manufacturers); and 3) keeping Quebec in Confederation – the clothing and textiles industries coincidentally being centred in Quebec. So our test does not prove the fixities hypothesis, although it does not disprove it, either.

The reimposing of the quota
In any event, the federal government reimposed barriers to imports of leather footwear, following intense lobbying by the shoe manufacturing industry. The reported rationale for the government's volte-face was an apparently unexpected increase in foreign competition from low-wage countries, such as Taiwan, Hong Kong, and Brazil, rather than from traditional sources of imported shoes, such as Italy and the eastern European countries. This all-too-familiar kind of story is consistent with the private-interest and rent-seeking theories of interventionist industrial policy-making and is surely not helpful to the fixities hypothesis.

There is, however, a further complicating factor. The government's decision to lift the import quotas in November 1981 came shortly after its tabling of a budget that gravely underestimated the depth of the coming recession. The decision to reintroduce the quotas came within two weeks of the tabling of a new budget, in June 1982, that accepted the fact of a deep recession and gave more emphasis to policies designed to raise employment than had the November 1981 budget. In other words, the recession may have made finding new employment in cities almost as difficult as in small towns. In that case, the decisions regarding the shoe and the clothing import quotas do not provide even a crude test of the fixities hypothesis.

Another question
A final point is that the test suggested here may have been framed incorrectly. We might have asked why import quotas have been applied to the footwear, clothing, and textile industries but to no others. One answer is that these industries are extremely susceptible to competition from foreign imports. But so are many other industries that must remain content with tariff protection alone. Another possibility is that the protected industries are among a small number of manufacturing industries whose economic characteristics (limited-scale economies, low transportation costs, and so on) permit them to locate in relatively small communities. In the light of the second answer, we can say that public policies towards the leather footwear, clothing, and textile industries appear at least consistent with the fixities hypothesis.

QUANTITATIVE STUDIES OF THE DETERMINANTS OF TARIFF PROTECTION AND INDUSTRIAL ASSISTANCE

The fixities hypothesis yields predictions that can be evaluated against evidence on the characteristics of industries or firms that receive government assistance or protection. The hypothesis suggests that the characteristics of industry structure (say, the concentration ratio) and performance (profitability or productivity) are less important determinants of assistance than the characteristics of the households whose workers supply their labour. In contrast, the rent-seeking or economic-theory-of-politics approach emphasizes structure and performance variables reflecting the ability to lobby for and retain aid and the industry's need for protection and assistance. (Of course, this test of the fixities hypothesis is applicable only if the characteristics of the industries receiving aid or protection match up with those that have work forces and locations for which fixities are likely to be important.)

Canadian evidence
To date, Canadian studies have focussed on a particular type of industrial assistance: effective tariff protection. Helleiner (1977) finds that although the level of effective protection was directly related to market concentration in 1961, no such relation appeared in 1970. According to Helleiner, by 1970 'the most significant explanatory variable in the Canadian tariff structure' is the degree to which the industry relies on unskilled labour (1977, 325). As we saw in Chapter 6, a high proportion of the net worth of low- and low-middle-income households consists of equity in a home. Thus, it seems likely that the workers in the industries receiving the most protection hold a high proportion of their assets in a form that is neither portable nor easily transferable in the event of plant closures. Moreover, since it seems safe to say that industries with large numbers of unskilled and relatively low-wage workers tend to be labour intensive with a low degree of factor specialization, the assistance these industries receive is presumably not necessitated by adjustment difficulties associated with a high proportion of fixed costs. Thus, it seems probable that the ultimate object of assistance is the work force, because it is the workers, not the firms for which they work, who are likely to encounter the greatest adjustment difficulties.

Some doubts about Helleiner's findings are raised in a recent study by Saunders (1980), which builds on an interest-group model developed by Caves (1976) to explain the pattern of tariff protection of Canada's secondary manufacturing industry. In the interest-group model, the demand for tariff protection is directly related to the potential benefits (rents) the protection creates, while the supply (by politicians) of protection is directly related to an industry's exposure to economic adversity. The former is assumed to depend on the level of industry concentration, while the latter is likely to generate sufficient equity claims in places with large numbers of low-skilled, low-wage workers. (Put this way, the supply side of the interest-group model is consistent with the fixities hypothesis.[3])

Saunders' model differs from that of Caves or Helleiner in two respects: 1) it includes several factors (foreign control, exports, an industry's labour productivity relative to that of its US counterpart) not accounted for in the other models; 2) it uses a two-stage least-squares estimation procedure to capture simultaneous-interaction or feedback effects neither of the others control for. (Simultaneity arises because some variables – concentration, productivity, foreign ownership, and exports – employed to explain the level of effective tariff protection are themselves influenced by the existence of high tariffs, according to the widely accepted Eastman-Stykolt [1967] model.[4])

Using the two-stage estimation procedure, Saunders finds the level of effective tariff protection related positively to the level of industry concentration (in contrast to the negative coefficient Caves obtains) and negatively related to foreign ownership and the percentage of industry shipments exported. To the extent that concentration brings with it lobbying strength (in the form of more funds and less of a free-rider problem), Saunders' finding is consistent with the private-interest–rent-seeking explanation for the distribution of effective protection. Saunders also finds a negative relationship between the level of effective tariff protection and the relative (Canada-to-US) labour-productivity variable. Since relative inefficiency is not necessarily the same thing as the low productivity associated with industries using relatively labour-intensive methods and large numbers of unskilled labourers, Saunders also controls for labour intensity and skill, but these variables turn out to be statistically insignificant.

Saunders' findings support theories emphasizing protection for industries that are economically inefficient but capable of wielding effective political power. For example, unprotected, inefficient industries are particularly susceptible to layoffs. However, Saunders' work is not particularly helpful to those who would like to find an equity rationale in the provision of effective tariff protection, although if the study had included nontariff barriers, it might have been easier for them to do so, as the examples of shoes and clothing suggest.

An Australian study

Kym Anderson carried out an interesting study on the determinants of all types of government assistance to Australian manufacturing industries. Like Helleiner, Anderson found that 'it is the labour-intensive, low wage industries with low value added shares of output that are the most highly assisted' (1980, 139). Like Caves (1976), however, Anderson uses a political model in which assistance is demanded and supplied. Thus, he interprets his finding that the industries with fewer firms receive more assistance as being consistent with the view that the fewer the firms the less likely are free-rider problems and therefore the greater the contribution to lobbying efforts (demand for assistance) by the industry group. Moreover, he explains the supply of assistance to low-wage, labour-intensive industries in terms of numbers of votes, although he notes that politicians 'rationalize' their actions in terms of social welfare. Thus, he concludes that his evidence marshals support for the economic theory of politics. Notice, however, that Anderson's findings are also at least partially consistent with those one would expect to find if fixities play a role in determining which industries receive industrial assistance.

A US study

Of the studies of the determinants of US tariff protection of which I am aware, the most thorough is a doctoral dissertation by Lavergne (1981). Obviously stimulated by the work of Helleiner, Caves, Saunders, Anderson, and others who have tested interest-group models, Lavergne goes to great pains to distil from a vast body of data the economic and political factors that underlie the US tariff structure. To do so, he tests six models of 'principled' tariff setting,[5] including the role of competitive disadvantages (or comparative costs), displacement costs, concessions in international bargaining sessions, the protection of defence-oriented industries, and the maintenance of competition in the US economy. Set against these is a pressure-group model designed to capture rent-seeking behaviour.

The hypotheses that receive the strongest support from Lavergne's regression analysis are that US tariff levels and structure are 1) positively related to an industry's comparative costs (and, therefore, to its susceptibility to competition from imports); 2) negatively related to the ability of the US government to extract bargaining concessions in international forums such as the Kennedy and Tokyo rounds; and 3) similar to what they were in 1930 or even 1900 – in other words, retention of the *status quo* is very important. He finds no evidence that tariffs are an arm of US competition policy or that they are used to protect defence-oriented industries, which apparently receive all the protection they need from nontariff barriers.

Lavergne's regression analysis provides little support for either the pressure-group model or the view that tariffs have been kept high in industries especially susceptible to high displacement costs. In fact, he concludes that tariff levels in the US reflect a combination of 'principled' tariff setting and the application of a conservative welfare function.[6]

Of particular interest to the present study is Lavergne's conclusion that his data support neither the pressure-group model nor the displacement-cost hypothesis. Since the pressure-group model is supposed to capture rent-seeking behaviour, lack of support for it is certainly consistent with the hypothesis that fixities in household production functions are an important ingredient in industrial policy-making.[7]

Lavergne's weak findings for the displacement effect are, on the face of it, much more difficult to rationalize. Further probing, however, suggests that they may not be inconsistent with the fixities hypothesis. Lavergne surmises that if displacement costs were important factors in tariff setting, industries with slow growth rates would suffer comparatively greater layoffs and reductions in capital values if tariffs were reduced. Thus, he employs an industry-growth variable to capture the role of the displacement effect, expecting that tariff levels would be negatively and significantly related to the industry-growth rate and that tariff reductions would be positively related. The regression analysis does not bear out these expectations. However, Lavergne also uses a variable that captures the extent to which employees in an industry reside outside metropolitan areas, and it is positively and significantly related to tariff levels, especially for industries that also receive nontariff protection. Lavergne makes rather little of this finding, perhaps regarding the variable as a weaker proxy for the size of the displacement effect than is the industry growth rate. However, if fixities in household production functions do influence tariff policy, and if, *ceteris parabis*, such fixities are more important in nonurban areas (where alternative employment opportunities are more limited), then the variable is a most relevant one and Lavergne's findings are potentially supportive of the fixities hypothesis.[8] In any event, Lavergne's study is not inconsistent with the view that economic exigency plays some role in industrial policy-making.

CONCLUSION

Evidence that industrial policies are actually influenced by the existence of household and local-government fixities is difficult to come by and tangential at best. Many protected industries hire labourers whose wealth is, in part, probably characterized by fixities, but it is not clear how important an influence on government policy this fact has been. While studies of industrial assistance provide evidence that is to a degree consistent with the fixities hypotheses, they also give some support to the alternative view that industries seek aid in relation to their need and their ability to benefit privately from it, and the same basis is largely the one on which the aid is, consciously or unconsciously, granted. Whether this behaviour represents rent-seeking or is only rent-maintaining is more difficult to discern. Moreover, the general conclusion is not necessarily inconsistent with the fixities hypothesis – but it is not obviously consistent either. Perhaps the most that can be said is that the existence of fixities may make a reversal of policy more difficult. That is, fixities may better explain the continuance of policies rather than their existence in the first place.[9]

At first blush, this result is disappointing. On further reflection, however, it is really not an unexpected finding. As noted in Chapter 1, both the rent-seeking and fixities hypothesis imply similar *political* behaviour. In addition, the *economic* data used in testing these hypotheses may simply not be adequate to allow the researcher to discriminate between the underlying stimuli, to say nothing of the difficulties in assessing the motives of political agents.

9
Summary and conclusions

The idea that fixities in household and government production functions may partly explain Canada's increasing reliance on interventionist industrial policies adds a new dimension to the study of the demand for such policies, a dimension that seems especially plausible in a nation whose land area in relation to its population is as great as ours. Although I have given little explicit attention to the actors who supply industrial policies, it seems clear that fixities in household and government production functions may produce economic exigency that adds a degree of immediacy and political legitimacy to governmental responses to requests for economic aid and protection. Vote-seeking legislators are not likely to be immune to demands for help from groups threatened with large and unrequited capital losses.[1]

SUMMARY

The fundamental point of this study is whether the growth of interventionist industrial policies is more a matter of self-seeking private-interest-group behaviour or, alternatively, whether it reflects the limitations of political institutions in dealing with economic exigency.

These interpretations are, of course, not mutually exclusive, but they are different. On the demand side there is a difference between seeking government's help to prevent unexpected losses and seeking assistance in generating or maintaining monopoly profits, transitory though they may be. On the supply side, there is a difference between political support in return for votes, financial support, and electoral footwork on one hand and political action to cope with what are accurately called 'people problems' on the other. At the level of perception, there is a difference between legislating economic privilege and preventing economic exigency. Unfortunately, the same means are often employed in both cases. Not surprisingly, the undesirable economic effects of one are also often those of the other.

Any complete, rigorous investigation of these alternative explanations of politicoeconomic behaviour would require a systematic examination of the history and the social and economic circumstances surrounding legislative and bureaucratic decision-making in Canada, a task well beyond the scope of this study. Instead, I have taken an indirect approach, focussing on the response to economic change and specifically on the idea that shifts in the amount and kinds of wealth held by individuals and households may affect their ability or willingness to adjust in the face of economic change.

Recall that a fundamental assumption of this study is that economic change is an ongoing process that produces some losers even in the best of circumstances. Given democratic political institutions and a pluralistic society, the losers, actual or potential, are likely to use 'voice' as well as 'exit' in response to adverse economic change. The economists' implicit assumption that mobility is *the* response to change is too limiting, particularly when it is a question of the geographic mobility of labour. Maximizing economic agents may 'stick' rather than 'switch' in the face of economic changes that call for a reallocation of resources. The fixities hypothesis helps to explain why: capital losses on nonportable, nontransferable assets may make it temporarily uneconomic for them to move, even if the return on their other assets, human and nonhuman, would be higher elsewhere. The use of 'voice' is the only apparent method of preventing or alleviating the impasse.

CONCLUSIONS

What conclusions can a study of this sort legitimately reach? The answer must be very tentative. Recall that I specified in the beginning that this work is intended as a positive study, one that attempts to explain how the world works, not a normative study of what should be. And at that level, I have at best presented a hypothesis without being able to test it more stringently than with intuition, casual empiricism, and a few case studies.

Consequently, my main conclusion can be only that the fixities hypothesis offers an interesting new dimension for the study of economic behaviour and political response. In recent years, the political economy of industrial policies has been dominated by analyses and arguments based on rent-seeking. In its political dimension, the fixities hypothesis extends the rent-seeking analysis to the case of negative rents and loss-avoidance. In its economic dimension, the hypothesis suggests that the conjunction of adverse economic change and the nonportability and nontransferability of certain household assets may combine not only to produce unrequited capital losses but to influence individual or household decisions to move. It is this behavioural response to the existence of fixities that gives the hypothesis economic relevance in the study of industrial policy.

This behavioural response may also allow me, very hesitantly, to suggest that the fixities phenomenon and the government actions it seems to have provoked are an example of a more general phenomenon. Whether the historical connection between industrial growth and the growth of democracy in the West is a coincidence or not, the two have produced an interesting tension. The industrial revolution and the economic growth that accompanied it required that resources move, in increasing amounts and with ever-greater speed, to new, more productive uses. Simultaneously, the rise of democratic institutions increased the possibility of the use of voice, providing an increase in nonmarket means of slowing down economic adjustments that may be socially efficient but are costly to some individuals. Thus, in an industrial democracy, the gap widens between what the economist can show to be efficient overall and the predictable behaviour of individual agents.

Normative ramifications
Although this study is positive in character, the subject of industrial policy has obvious normative ramifications. Does the fixities hypothesis have normative implications? Here, I believe, we encounter dangers as well as difficulties. Those people who argue that equity should stand alongside efficiency in the evaluation of industrial policies will find in the fixities hypothesis an added case for interventionism. The case in equity for protection against uncontrolled and unrequited capital losses will seem to them at least as good as the case for reducing inequalities in income flows. On the other hand, those economists who evaluate industrial policies on efficiency grounds alone will give little or no weight to economic exigency created by fixities. Fixities may result in changes in capital values, but except to the extent that they retard migration, they do not alter the parameters of efficiency.

I am inclined to align with the latter group for two reasons. First, for methodological reasons I do not think that equity considerations can be successfully introduced into formal economic evaluations of desirable or undesirable policies. Any policy produces winners and losers, and unless society assigns weights to each group, economists are in no position to choose among them. Of course, losers can be compensated, and, in principle, the economic policies that are socially beneficial are the ones under which the beneficiaries should be willing to compensate the losers fully. In practice, such compensation is rarely envisaged, much less offered, in part because any attempt to do so might involve transactions costs so substantial that the net benefits of many programs would be greatly reduced, if not eliminated (Quinn and Trebilcock 1982).

My second objection to giving fixities much normative weight in designing government policies is more fundamental. Recall that one reason risk-averting economic agents usually choose organized political activity rather than insurance in the face of risks from adverse economic change is that insurance is either unavailable or very costly. A major source of the problem is moral hazard – the very fact of insurance coverage alters actuarial values by giving insured parties an incentive to consume more of the covered activity or to undertake greater risks than they otherwise would. In other words, if government compensates, bails out, or protects actual or prospective losers from economic change, economic agents will take fewer steps to avoid being losers. They may accept socially unacceptable risks, knowing that government stands ready to prevent or absorb losses. Whether the government tool is interventionist industrial policies or lump-sum compensation payments, economic agents will have an incentive to make inefficient choices and avoid efficient, but costly, reallocations of resources.[2]

A CLOSING WORD

Where does the clash between positive and normative analysis leave us? No thoughtful advocate of capitalism or free enterprise has ever denied that economic progress would produce some (temporary?) losers. The dilemma is whether the state should respond – and how. As it turns out, not responding is likely to be politically self-defeating. A democratic society permits free association; there is no constitutional restraint preventing losers (or winners) from banding together and lobbying in their own interests. The problem is that the results of successful lobbying efforts almost always include some form of protection from the operation of market forces. Thus, although some economists (for example, Hayek [1973] and Friedman [1962]) have argued that economic freedom is fundamental to a truly democratic society, democratic institutions, in the absence of any constitutional restraints to the contrary, will predictably behave so as to restrict economic freedom.

Thus, this study ends on an agnostic note. At the level of positive economics, I have suggested that the very growth in affluence generates strong pressures for the growth of interventionist industrial policies, yet I have not been able to test this hypothesis rigorously. At the normative level, the fixities hypothesis has implications that will make life more complicated for economists seeking rational and objective evaluations of economic policy. Realistically, this study only begins to develop a broader framework within which to understand *why* government so frequently intervenes in the economy and a source of the pressure to intervene. If the main hypothesis is sufficiently interesting to spur other economists to make further attempts to test it, the study will have accomplished one of its primary purposes.

Appendix
Interventionist policies versus tax-transfer systems

Although I would downplay the normative aspect of the fixities hypothesis, I believe the distributional issues it raises throw light on the choice of redistributional policies our society actually employs. Specifically, why has government responded to distributional concerns with interventionist industrial policies rather than with an income-transfer program such as a negative tax plan? The question is an important one since economists usually argue that if economic exigency exists, the solution lies in the tax-transfer system rather than in attempts to control price and/or output by market intervention. The latter, besides being inefficient, produces redistributions of income that violate the accepted principles of horizontal equity; market intervention rarely gives equal treatment to equals.

A possible explanation for the choice of interventionist industrial policies over tax-transfer schemes in cases of economic exigency is that the former give weight to changes in relative as well as absolute income. Suppose, for example, an economic change reduces person (or family) X's income from 10 to 5 while Y's income remains at 5. A negative income tax plan keyed to the positions of X and Y after the change would treat them identically. (If income were averaged, X would actually get less than Y.) But suppose that society feels that in addition to considering the *level* of a person's income, it should also give some weight to large negative *changes* in the income or wealth of nonrich persons, at least to those changes over which the people involved have no control.[1] Then, when X's income falls from 10 to 5, society may believe that X is deserving of more support than Y, whose low income remains at 5.[2] Since a negative income tax plan does not distinguish X and Y, government policy might respond by protecting X's occupation or industry in an attempt to reduce the decline in his or her income. In other words, society does not consider or treat X and Y as equals for distributive purposes.[3]

Table A.1 illustrates what I have in mind. Column 1 gives the initial

TABLE A.1
Effects of NIT and government intervention after economic change

Person	Initial position		Position after economic change		Change in income or wealth		Position after government intervention[a]		Change from initial position		Change from position after economic change	
	Pre-NIT	Post-NIT	Pre-NIT	Post-NIT	Pre-NIT (3) - (1)	Post-NIT (4) - (2)	Pre-NIT	Post-NIT	Pre-NIT (7) - (1)	Post-NIT (8) - (2)	Pre-NIT (7) - (3)	Post-NIT (8) - (4)
	(1)	(2)	(3)	(4)	(5)	(6)	(7)	(8)	(9)	(10)	(11)	(12)
A	26	23	23	21	-3	-2	22.5	21.0	-3.5	-2.0	-0.5	0
B	20	18	24	22	+4	+4	23.5	22.0	+3.5	+4.0	-0.5	0
C	18	16	20	19	+2	+3	19.5	18.5	+1.5	+2.5	-0.5	-0.5
D	16	15	10	11	-6	-4	13.0	13.0	-3.0	-2.0	+3.0	+2.0
E	10	11	12	12	+2	+1	11.5	11.5	+1.5	+0.5	-0.5	-0.5
F	8	10	10	11	+2	+1	9.5	10.5	+1.5	+0.5	-0.5	-0.5
G	2	7	6	9	+4	+2	5.5	8.5	+3.5	+1.5	0	-0.5
Sum	100	100	105	105	+5	+5	105.0	105.0	+5.0	+5.0	0	0
Range[b]	24	16	18	13	|10|	|8|	18.0	13.5	|7.0|	|6.5|		

NOTE: NIT payment $= r(B - Y)$, for Y B where B = breakeven level of income (= 12) and r = negative tax rate = 0.5. An arbitrary set of taxes is imposed on persons with Y B to pay for the NIT.

[a] Government intervenes to protect D's market position so that the price of what D sells is higher than it would otherwise be. Real incomes of all other persons are assumed to be reduced by 0.5. Position is now based on incomes after the economic change, as in columns (3) and (4).

[b] Highest income minus lowest income.

income positions of persons A through G before negative income tax payments. Column 2 shows their positions after those with incomes of less than 12 receive NIT payments, and those whose incomes exceed 12 pay taxes to provide the transfers. Columns 3 and 4 indicate what happens to pre- and post-transfer incomes as a result of an economic change.[4] The spotlight falls on person D, whose income has fallen from 16 to 10. He is now worse off than person E and no better off than person F, whose pre-transfer income before the economic change was half that of person D. The negative income tax helps person D a little but leaves his worsened relative position unchanged. D and F are treated identically under the NIT.

If society believes that past positions also count (or sometimes count), it may be prepared to give special aid to person D. The result is shown in Column 7: a price support or subsidy policy partially offsets D's fall in income. To pay for the aid, all the others pay somewhat higher prices and/or taxes (reducing their real and/or disposable incomes). D's original relative position is restored, and his income level raised above post-change levels, although with an income of 13 he is no longer eligible for NIT.

It is perhaps noteworthy that, by complementing the NIT, the interventionist policy reduces the dispersion in income changes – compare Columns 9 and 10 with Columns 5 and 6 – but does not materially reduce the decline in inequality produced by the economic change. Of course, this result reflects the way in which the example is constructed, but it might be quite general, particularly if interventionist policies favour the middle or lower classes rather than the rich. Also no consideration is given to the loss in the value of output produced as a result of allocative inefficiency of the interventionist policy.

Not all declines in income may matter in the sense of prompting interventionist policies. For example, in Table A.1 the economic change caused a substantial decline in the income of person A, who lost position relative to B. Yet no attention was given to this change. Why? I suppose that when the rich change their incomes and relative ranks, no one (but them) really cares. What about the other extreme? Suppose there were a person H whose initial pre-transfer income of 3 fell to 1 after the economic change. Why does the example give no attention to this possibility? The answer probably is that since H's income is already very low, it cannot fall much further.[5] Moreover, H would already be receiving very substantial help from the NIT transfers, and that assistance would rise with the pre-transfer income loss.

The overall implication is that interventionist industrial policies will be mainly aimed at protecting the incomes (and wealth) of the middle- and lower-middle-income classes, groups whose wealth is most likely to include fixities.[6]

Notes

CHAPTER 1

1 This is not to imply that government intervention was negligible before the 1930s, only that it has significantly increased since then.

2 The term 'industrial policy' has no precise, generally agreed-on meaning. It can be construed narrowly or broadly. I incline towards the latter, whereby industrial policies can be thought of as any programs of government that relate directly to the economic activity of one or more of a nation's regions, industries, firms, or plants. Industrial policies may be of an interventionist or a noninterventionist character (although there is a natural, and perhaps unfortunate, tendency to define them in terms of the former to the exclusion of the latter). Interventionist industrial policies involve relatively direct control over the way in which resources are allocated and may be broadly divided into three types: those that promote growth and development; those that protect against changes and/or decline; and those that aid the adjustment or reallocation of resources away from economically declining activities. Noninterventionist industrial policies usually rely on the market to direct the allocation of resources; they may be of the 'hands-off' sort (for example, a policy of free trade or a refusal to enforce contracts in restraint of trade), or they may set 'rules of the game' (for example, competition policy).

3 Musgrave (1959) has characterized the government's public finance role as consisting of three branches: allocation, distribution, and stabilization.

4 For a comprehensive discussion of rent-seeking, see Hartle (1983).

5 Students of the literature on economic regulation will recognize the similarity between my terminology and that of Stigler (1971). It will become apparent, however, that although I am sympathetic to Stigler's argument, at least with respect to its explanation of government intervention in certain industries, I do not find it exhaustive. Moreover, it does not explain why intervention has apparently increased.

6 Both views assume that governments are reacting to societal preferences or pressures. In contrast, some political scientists hold that government officials may unilaterally initiate some public programs and policies in response to state rather than societal preferences (Nordlinger 1981).

7 For a related but somewhat different approach that focusses on regulation as a conflict-resolution process, see Hartle (1979).

8 The bridge between these two views is, I suppose, provided by rent-maintaining behaviour.

9 Recall my statement that the hypothesis examined in this study is at most a *partial* explanation for the growth of interventionist industrial policies. Undoubtedly, a number of valid explanations exist. In particular, I want to underline that I have no intention of treating the rent-seeking and economic-exigency hypotheses as competing, testing one against the other. Each, in my view, is capable of explaining some observed behaviour of economic and political agents.

10 The political dangers are brilliantly demonstrated and analysed in Usher (1981).

11 For an elaboration, see North (1978).

CHAPTER 2

1 My view of capitalism is quite Schumpeterian (1950). See also Nelson and Winter (1982).

2 For this and other reasons, Nelson (1981) argues that a persuasive case for private enterprise cannot rest on the analytical basis provided by modern welfare economics.

3 Baldwin and Gorecki (1983), using newly available data, recently calculated the average number of entrants to and exits from 141 manufacturing industries between 1970 and 1979. On average about 25 per cent of the establishments assigned to these industries in 1979 had been 'born' during the preceding decade and about a third of those in existence in 1970 had been scrapped by 1979.

4 Usher (1981) argues the dangers to the continued existence of democracy if legislatures attempt to 'assign' incomes.

CHAPTER 3

1 Compare wage and salary data for various industries and occupations in different cities, as reported in Canada (1982a).

2 Rigid wages in the presence of less than fully mobile labour may, in theory, provide a rationale for using an output subsidy to protect an industry that has lost its international competitiveness (Rees and Forster 1981). This argument is a classic example of the theory of the second best: once an inefficient government policy is introduced and is taken as given, then a second-best solution may be to introduce another inefficient government policy, in this case protection. This study, however, does not rely on the much-overworked theory of the second best. Rather, it suggests that even in the absence of inefficient government policies, certain economic changes may contribute to reducing mobility and thereby to increasing the *demand* for protectionist industrial policies.

3 Although observed labour mobility remains high in both Canada and the US and there is as yet little definitive evidence that private pension plans have actually reduced mobility, particularly among younger workers, the potential for their inducing immobility is clearly there, as demonstrated in Chapter 6. Moreover, to the extent that mobility remains high and is largely unaffected by pension plans, it follows that many years of service are lost so far as pension benefits are concerned (Prefontaine and Balcer 1979).

CHAPTER 4

1 'Transferability' refers here to the possibility of exchange, which depends not only on legal conditions but also on the thickness or thinness of the market for the asset involved.

2 Williamson (1981), writing within a transactions-cost framework, develops the concept of 'asset specificity', which he defines as arising from site specificity, physical specificity, or human-asset specificity. Durability and transactions-specificity characterize investments with asset-specific characteristics. According to Williamson, asset specificity implies that once investments are made, 'buyer and seller are effectively operating in a bilateral-exchange relation for a considerable period thereafter' (p.1546). Thus, as assets become more specific, market contracting becomes less efficient and internal organization tends to displace markets (p.1548). Earlier, DiVanzo (1977, 67) used the term 'location specific capital' to refer to assets that are more valuable in their current location than they would be in other areas. Thus, location-specific capital includes such things as personal ties and relationships, information about the labour and product markets, clientele, and seniority, as well as the family's home. For an interesting Canadian study in which location-specific capital looms large, see Norrie and Percy (1983).

   The reader may ask why I have not simply relied on the concept of asset specificity and dispensed with the theoretical analysis that takes up much of this chapter. My answer is that it is desirable to embed responses to asset specificities in the theory of household behaviour.

3 The impact of family ties on migration decisions can also be analysed within an explicitly economic framework that assumes maximizing behaviour (Mincer 1978). So can language factors. In fact, Becker (1975) argues that economic tools can be used to analyse even specifically noneconomic influences.

4 Krashinsky, following Lancaster (1966), gives a particularly clear example of household production: 'consumption is a two-stage process: the consumer purchases goods and services; he then uses his expertise and time to combine these purchases to produce "characteristics".... he combines purchased food, electricity, and a kitchen to produce "supper"' (1981, 31).

5 Moreover, the nature of some common household assets, such as a house, is such that accepting a sizeable decline in wages may make holding onto it or maintaining its service value all but impossible.

6 See Sandell (1977) for an analysis of the impact of the wife's labour-market involvement on a family's decision to migrate.

7 We have here one reason why households may borrow to the hilt. So long as equity is limited and indebtedness great, a household loses relatively little if it must adjust (move), because it can simply turn the asset *cum* liability (for example, a house with a mortgage) over to the bank, finance company, or other creditor.

8 Notice that the fixities hypothesis has much in common with Mishkin's (1977) liquidity hypothesis, which stresses the importance of the *composition* of the household's balance sheet has for its decisions on consumer expenditures. Mishkin distinguishes between household assets and liabilities (rather than netting the latter out against the former) and focusses on the fact that imperfect capital markets make certain tangible consumer assets highly illiquid. The household that attempts to sell them quickly for cash may incur capital losses. Thus, in a time of economic exigency (such as the recession in the United States in 1974-5, which was the subject of Mishkin's study), financial stress

causes a large decline in the purchase of tangible assets. Financial stress is produced when the value of the consumer's financial assets is low relative to his or her liabilities (specifically, debt service on consumer durables, including housing). A deep recession that reduces the household's income, its financial assets, and the market value of tangible assets leads to belt-tightening in an attempt to hold on to existing assets against which consumer debt is writ large. While Mishkin's study says nothing about mobility as such, one could interpret his hypothesis as relating to the impact of economic exigency and financial stress on consumption mobility – that is, on the ability of the consumer to move among tangible assets.

9 For US farms, Weiss (1980) estimates that, on average, 50 per cent of costs are fixed, and that some of what are treated as variable costs would be more properly considered overhead costs.

10 Olson (1964) explicitly recognizes that attaching importance to local reputation and status implies the interdependence of utility functions. Bird and Hartle (1972), in a paper that attempts to explain localism or regionalism, handle reputation and prestige in an analogous manner.

CHAPTER 5

1 Of course, not all of this government growth involves production or consumption on behalf of citizens; much of it reflects transfers between different levels of government and between governments and individuals.

2 Notice that the argument here does not depend on whether the capital intensity of the government sector is greater or less than that of the private sector, or on whether the capital intensity of the government sector has risen or fallen over time – both interesting questions in other contexts. In fact, Bird (1979) reviews evidence that suggests the federal government is more capital-intensive than the private sector but is becoming relatively less so. The government sector's capital-employment ratio has declined in the last two decades, but almost all of the decrease is attributable to changes at the federal government level. The provincial and municipal governments are the most capital-intensive parts of the public sector, and their capital intensity does not appear to have declined significantly during the postwar period (Bird 1979, 119).

3 The argument here is similar to that of Buchanan and Goetz (1972) and Flatters, Henderson, and Mieszkowski (1974): perfect labour mobility between regions is inefficient if local taxes are used to finance local public goods. When migrants make the decision to move, they do not include in their calculus that their leaving reduces the tax base and the ability to finance public goods in the region they leave or that their arrival broadens the tax base and lightens the tax load of the region in which they settle. In a sense, their mobility creates an externality. For a contrasting view, see Usher (1977).

4 It should be noted, however, that a substantial portion of municipal revenues comes from provincial grants. What percentage of these transfers covers capital expenditures is unclear, although the issue is important.

5 Buchanan and Goetz (1972) make this point forcefully.

6 In fact, even if household fixities inhibit the geographic mobility of labour, it is possible that, given fixities in government production functions, the actual level of migration may exceed the optimal level, rather than fall below it.

    For another explanation of why the actual level of migration may exceed the optimal level, see Boadway and Flatters (1982).

CHAPTER 6

1   Although wealth statistics usually show that wealth is more unequally distributed than income, the data here show that the disparity may be smaller when one considers both income and wealth.
2   To be sure, housing values have declined sharply in many areas in the last few years, thus suggesting that equity in a home is now a somewhat smaller share of household wealth than it was in the 1970s. Nevertheless, it is highly unlikely that housing values, on the whole, have fallen enough to qualify my argument to any significant degree.
3   These ratios are probably exaggerated by the fact that the net worth figures do not include wealth in the form of private pension plan claims.
4   The figures in Table 9 raise a question about the nexus between home ownership, age, and mobility. It is well known that home ownership and age are directly related, with the highest incidence of home ownership (74 per cent in 1977) occurring in the 45-to-54 age group with the 35-to-44 and 55-to-64 groups not far behind (Canada 1979b, table 3). Moreover, economic theory predicts, and the evidence confirms, that job mobility and age are inversely related because the prospective gains from changing jobs decline with the number of years of working life remaining (Courchene 1970; Vanderkamp and Grant 1976). The age factor does not, however, explain the high incidence of home ownership in the Atlantic provinces since the percentages of their population in 35-to-44, 45-to-54, and 55-to-64 age groups are actually lower than the percentages for Canada as a whole. By the same token, age cannot be a significant factor in explaining why the income and earnings differentials between the Atlantic provinces and the rest of Canada do not produce the migration differentials theory predicts (Courchene 1970). This phenomenon does not, of course, prove that home ownership is the explanation since other factors, such as government policies, particularly transfer-payment programs, may have retarded migration from Atlantic Canada. (See, for example, Foot and Milne [1981] and Winer and Gauthier [1982].) One of the few studies of the impact of home ownership on migration – and one that suggests home ownership may somewhat retard migration – is Lansing and Mueller (1967, chap. 6).
5   Presumably, lenders (creditors) would have taken expected losses fully into account and reflected them in mortgage rates, low limits on the percentage of homeowner equity, and so on. However, borrowers (prospective homeowners) may not take the possibility of capital losses *fully* into account because of well-known asymmetries of information in the housing market and/or because of a belief that legislatures can be counted on to respond to economic exigency with some form of rescue operation. Moreover, trust companies and banks, which hold most mortgages, have far more diversified portfolios than do mortgagees and, therefore, are much less likely to suffer real economic exigency when house values in a particular location fall precipitously.

CHAPTER 7

1   Presumably, one result is that the firm pays lower wages or lower taxes than it would otherwise pay. In effect, the risks of capital losses caused by fixities are socialized – that

is, spread over all members, present or future, of the relevant groups.

2 The extent to which Eldorado accepted or followed the consultant's recommendations is not clear.

3 I am indebted to Professor John Bradbury of the Department of Geography, McGill University, for letting me use an unpublished study (1982), from which all the figures reported here are drawn.

4 Note that there is very little equity built up in the first five or even ten years of a thirty-year mortgage.

5 Actually, some of the costs and the risks are transferred to the federal government – and the taxpayers at large – via the tax system, particularly the capital cost allowance rules whereby mining firms have been able to write off a great deal of the cost of preparing housing sites and developing transport systems in remote areas. The old three-year exemption of income from new mines was also helpful in this respect. There is also some socialization of risk on the wage side via tax-free allowances for workers. (I am indebted to Richard M. Bird for bringing these points to my attention.)

6 Here again the tax system plays a role because it substantially favours employees who work only temporarily at remote mining sites (see Bird and Slack 1983).

7 I am indebted to Professor David Laidler for suggesting that studies involving council housing could prove useful examples of some of the problems investigated in the present study.

8 The growing prevalence of rent control in Canada's larger cities suggests that the fixities associated with housing, and their potential for reducing or slowing down mobility, are not limited to or even necessarily concentrated in small towns and rural areas.

9 Occasionally, a long-term tenant is able to purchase a council house outright. Although such purchases are a privilege, not a right, apparently a substantial number of local authority houses have been sold to sitting tenants (Murie, Niner, and Watson 1976, 5).

10 Predictably, occupants of private rental housing had higher migration rates than owner-occupiers (Hughes and McCormick 1981, 935).

11 The local environment is, of course, a fixity as defined in this study. It is a good that, combined with other goods and particularly leisure, produces utility for individuals, and it is neither transferable nor portable.

12 At the time Langbaurgh, the housing area serving South Teesside, had more than 6000 applications for accommodation, and a Hartlepool Council tenant who applied for housing there was almost certain to be assigned a low place on the waiting list because priority was being given to people already living in Langbaurgh, the elderly, sub-tenants, and tenants in overcrowded accommodations or those lacking basic amenities (Smith 1978, 66-7).

13 The author of the Hartlepool study cautions, however, that the respondents' answers to questions about the ease or difficulty of finding suitable housing elsewhere reflected their perceptions, not fact. Actually, there were few council-housing vacancies and many cases of long waiting lists in areas where jobs existed. Thus, some of the would-be migrants would probably not have moved once they learned of council-housing restrictions elsewhere.

14 Presumably, the choice of not moving is made tenable by the availability of unemployment insurance and welfare payments for persons out of work or in economic need.

15 The average wage at the Plainfield plant was about $3.50 per hour compared to $2.50 at Hagerstown, where unemployment was very high.

16 Losses would have come from some influence on the market other than the Mack closure; New Jersey is an almost solidly urbanized area with few of the characteristics of a single-sector community.

17 Currently, for workers with the minimum insured weeks (twenty), the payout period ranges from twenty weeks if the regional unemployment rate is less than 4 per cent to forty-two weeks if the rate is greater than 11.5 per cent.

18 The UIC variable also included the ratio of initial claims accepted to initial claims filed, a crude attempt at measuring interprovincial differences in the strictness with which UIC eligibility rules are applied (Winer and Gauthier 1982, 33).

19 It should be noted, however, that under most trade union pension plans, the workers do not make any contributions. Thus, their mobility decisions should not be influenced by the prospect of 'lock-in'.

20 Professor James Pesando tells me that prospective pension reforms will probably eliminate the age requirement for vesting and reduce the required service to five or even three years.

21 For some observers this fact provides an efficiency argument for immediate vesting or at least a less stringent rule then '45 and 10'. Moreover, since private pension plans are widely viewed as a form of deferred wages (Rea and Pesando [1980], chap. 2; see Asimakopulos and Weldon [1970] for another view), the failure to vest benefits automatically is seen as inequitable. Becker (1964) has argued, however, that delayed vesting may be viewed as a way in which firms share with their employees the costs of firm-specific training.

22 With a flat earnings profile, the respective benefit-to-contribution ratios would be 1.4 and 2.2. (I am indebted to Professor A. Asimakopulos for bringing these figures to my attention.)

23 But if job mobility leads to higher earnings, to say nothing of greater satisfaction, the pension-related losses associated with job mobility will be offset by other gains, pecuniary and nonpecuniary.

24 It is also worth noting that much of the past thirty years' growth in private-pension-plan coverage (see Table 12) reflects the increase in public-sector employment. In 1947, the approximately 600,000 private-sector members of private pension plans constituted almost three-quarters of all plan members. In 1976 almost half (45 per cent) of the private-pension-plan membership of 3.9 million were public-sector employees (Canada 1979c, vol. 1, p. 39).

25 There is something of a paradox here. The optimal-labour-contracts theory argues that deferred vesting is designed to reduce mobility in order to cover firm-specific training costs. Yet the explanation for why so few plans are vested is that mobility is so high. Actually, what now appears to be of more concern is the possibility that the firm will go bankrupt, leaving vested pension liabilities inadequately funded. On the risk of bankruptcy in pension plans, see Pesando (1982).

CHAPTER 8

1 The extent of job loss, however, is in question. See Jenkins (1981).

2 In comparison, in 1974, there were thirty-six smaller communities with a footwear plant (Canada 1978, 5).

3 Saunders, in conversation, agreed with this interpretation.

4 According to Eastman and Stykolt (1967), tariff protection attracts foreign direct investment and sustains inefficiently scaled producers thereby depressing the level of exports, productivity, and concentration.

5 'Principled' apparently means set on some objective basis, as opposed to an 'ad hoc' structure that simply reflects the strength of particular interest groups.

6 The conservative welfare function incorporates the 'principle' that significant reductions in the income of any major group should be avoided so that 'no social groups should be forced to suffer excessive losses' (Lavergne 1981, 527). See Corden (1974). As Lavergne notes, the problem with the conservative welfare function is the weak support he finds for the role of displacement costs.

7 As Lavergne admits, however, several of his variables may be proxies for interest-group pressures. This is particularly true in testing the comparative-cost hypothesis since a positive relationship between tariff levels and cost disadvantages may reflect the fact that the net gains from protection tend to increase with the susceptibility to competition. Nevertheless, Lavergne could find little evidence that either industry concentration (a proxy for the ability to retain gains from increased protection) or the extent of unionization, two of the leading pressure-group variables, is positively related to the level of US tariffs.

8 Nevertheless, in subsequent work (1983) Lavergne is dubious about the meaning of the relationship between his RURAL variable and the tariff-level variable.

9 This conclusion is quite consistent with Lavergne's (1981) emphasis on the conservative welfare function.

CHAPTER 9

1 In fact, in some cases, what appears to be rent-seeking or rent-maintaining behaviour may be an attempt by an economic agent(s) to prevent capital losses unrequited by any previous (or expected future) capital gain. This case would occur once existing rents are dissipated by the costs of rent-seeking behaviour (Posner 1975) or have been capitalized into the sale price of a rent-generating asset (including a licence, quota, or other restriction on entry into a profitable trade, occupation, or industry) so that a subsequent purchaser may be receiving only normal returns from the asset prior to the adverse economic change. Tullock (1975) aptly terms the resulting political conundrum the 'transitional gains trap'.

2 Although interventionist industrial policies might involve greater gross inefficiencies than a program of lump-sum compensation payments, the latter would also be costly. Specifically, it would require raising taxes, and as Usher (1982) shows, the marginal cost of public funds is substantially greater than one.

APPENDIX

1 The Canada and Quebec Pension Plans and Unemployment Insurance give some attention to the latter objective.

2   The concern with the change may be no less great if X's previous position was attributable in part to economic rents generated by an inefficient government policy such as import and export quotas or subsidies. In this case, treating X differently from Y is an example of a rent-maintaining policy.

3   Since X and Y may not be equals in the eyes of society, their different treatment does not necessarily violate the principles of horizontal equity. The consideration that they are not equals can be understood in terms of the conservative welfare function. See Corden (1974), as well as Lavergne's (1981) empirical investigation, which supports the major hypothesis suggested by that form of the welfare function.

4   Note that the economic change increases aggregate income (produces growth) and *reduces* the dispersion (inequality?) of incomes as measured by the range of income.

5   If we exclude the possibility of negative income. Of course, negative wealth (liabilities exceed assets) is a real possibility.

6   This conclusion is consistent with the hypothesis of Aaron Director; see Stigler (1970) and Peltzman (1980).

Bibliography

Anderson, Kym (1980) 'The political market for government assistance to Australian manufacturing' *The Economic Record* 56: 132-44

Asimakopulos, A., and J.C. Weldon (1970) 'On private plans in the theory of pensions' *Canadian Journal of Economics* 3: 223-37

Baldwin, J., and P. Gorecki (1983) 'Entry and exit in the Canadian manufacturing sector: 1970-1979'. Economic Council of Canada Discussion Paper 225 (Ottawa: February)

Becker, Gary S. (1964) *Human Capital* (New York: National Bureau of Economic Research)

– (1965) 'A theory of the allocation of time' *Economic Journal* 75: 493-517

– (1975) *Economic Theory* (Chicago: University of Chicago Press)

Bird, Richard M. (1979) *The Growth of Public Employment in Canada* (Toronto: Butterworth for the Institute for Research on Public Policy)

Bird, R.M., and D.G. Hartle (1972) 'The demand for local political autonomy: an individualistic theory' *Journal of Conflict Resolution* 15 (4): 443-6

Bird, R.M., and N.E. Slack (1983) 'The taxation of northern allowances' *Canadian Tax Journal* 31 (September–October): 783-96

Bliss, Michael (1982) 'The evolution of industrial policies in Canada: an historical survey'. Economic Council of Canada Discussion Paper 218 (Ottawa: June)

Boadway, Robin, and Frank Flatters (1982) 'Efficiency and equalization payments in a federal system of government: a synthesis and extension of recent results' *The Canadian Journal of Economics* 15 (November): 613-33

Bradbury, John (1982) 'Mining communities in the Quebec-Labrador iron ore trough' (Montreal: McGill University, October). Mimeo

Buchanan, J.M., and Charles J. Goetz (1972) 'Efficiency limits of fiscal mobility' *Journal of Public Economics* 1 (April): 25-43

Buchanan, J.M., G. Tullock, and R.D. Tollison, eds. (1981) *Toward a Theory of the Rent Seeking Society* (College Station: Texas A&M University Press)

Bucovetsky, M.W. (1975) 'The mining industry and the great tax reform debate'. In A. Paul Pross, ed., *Pressure Group Behaviour in Canadian Politics* (Toronto: McGraw-Hill Ryerson)

Canada (1955) Statistics Canada. *Income, Assets and Indebtedness of Non-Farm Families in Canada* cat. 13-508 (Ottawa)

– (1958) Statistics Canada. *Income, Assets and Indebtedness of Non-Farm Families in Canada* cat. 13-514 (Ottawa)

– (1966) Statistics Canada. *Income, Assets and Indebtedness of Families in Canada* cat. 13-525 (Ottawa)

– (1973) Statistics Canada. *Income, Assets and Indebtedness of Families in Canada* cat. 13-547 occasional (Ottawa)

– (1978) Department of Industry, Trade and Commerce. *Canada's Footwear Industry: Sector Profile* (Ottawa)

– (1979a) Department of Regional Economic Expansion. *Single Sector Communities* DREE occasional paper (Ottawa: Supply and Services Canada)

– (1979b) Statistics Canada. *Home Ownership and Mortgage Debt in Canada, 1977* Consumer Income and Expenditure Division (Ottawa: July)

– (1979c) Task Force on Retirement Income Policy. *The Retirement Income System in Canada: Problems and Alternative Policies for Reform* (Ottawa: Supply and Services Canada)

– (1980) Statistics Canada. *Income, Assets and Indebtedness of Families in Canada* cat. 13-572 occasional (Ottawa)

–(1981a) *Local Government Finance* cat. 68-204 (Ottawa)

–(1981b) Statistics Canada. *Mergers, Plant Openings and Closings of Large Transnational and Other Enterprises* cat. 75-507 occasional (Ottawa)

– (1982a) Labour Canada. *Wage Rates, Salaries, Hours of Labour 1981* (Ottawa)

– (1982b) Statistics Canada. *Pension Plans in Canada* cat. 74-401 biennial (Ottawa)

Canadian Textile Journal (1977) *Manual of the Textile Industry of Canada, 1977* 49th annual edition (Montreal)

Caves, Richard E. (1976) 'Economic models of political choice: Canada's tariff structure' *Canadian Journal of Economics* 9 (May): 278-300

Corden, Max (1974) *Trade Policy and Economic Welfare* (Oxford: Clarendon Press)

Courchene, Thomas (1970) 'Interprovincial migration and economic adjustment' *Canadian Journal of Economics* 3 (November): 550-75
- (1974) *Migration, Income and Employment in Canada 1965-68* (Montreal: C.D. Howe Institute)
- (1980) 'Towards a protected society: the politicization of economic life' *Canadian Journal of Economics* 13 (November)
Davenport, P., C. Green, W. Milne, R. Saunders, and W.G. Watson (1982) *Industrial Policy in Ontario and Quebec* (Toronto: Ontario Economic Council)
DiVanzo, Julie (1977) *Why Families Move: A Model of the Geographic Mobility of Married Couples* US Department of Labor, Employment and Training Administration, R&D Monograph 48 (Washington: US Government Printing Office)
Dorsey, John W. (1967) 'The Mack case: a study in unemployment'. In Otto Eckstein, ed., *Studies in the Economics of Income Maintenance* (Washington: The Brookings Institution)
Eastman, H., and S. Stykolt (1967) *The Tariff and Competition in Canada* (Toronto: Macmillan of Canada)
Fields, Gary (1979) 'Place-to-place migration: some new evidence' *Review of Economics and Statistics* 61 (February): 21-32
Flatters, Frank R., J.V. Henderson, and Peter Mieszkowski (1974) 'Public goods, efficiency, and regional fiscal equalization' *Journal of Public Economics* 3 (May): 99-112
Foot, David, and William Milne (1981) 'Public policies and interprovincial migration in Canada: an econometric analysis'. Institute for Policy Analysis, University of Toronto, working paper 8126 (September)
Forbes, J.D., R.D. Hughes, and T.K. Warley (1982) *Economic Intervention and Regulation in Canadian Agriculture* Economic Council of Canada and Institute for Research on Public Policy (Ottawa: Supply and Services Canada)
Friedman, Milton (1962) *Capitalism and Freedom* (Chicago: University of Chicago Press)
Gray, Hamish (1968) *The Cost of Council Housing* (London: Institute of Economic Affairs)
Green, Christopher (1983) 'Agricultural marketing boards in Canada: an economic and legal analysis' *University of Toronto Law Journal* 33 (fall): 407-33
Greenwood, M. (1975) 'Research on internal migration in the United States: a survey' *Journal of Economic Literature* 13 (June): 397-433
Grubel, H.G. (1982) 'Reflections on a Canadian bill of economic rights'

Canadian Public Policy 8 (1, winter): 57-68

Hartle, Douglas (1979) *Public Policy Decision Making and Regulation* (Montreal: Institute for Research on Public Policy)

– (1983) 'The theory of "rent-seeking": some reflections' *Canadian Journal of Economics* 16 (November): 539-54

Hayek, F.A. (1945) 'The use of knowledge in society' *The American Economic Review* 35 (September): 519-30

– (1960) *The Constitution of Liberty* (London and Chicago: Regnery)

– (1973) *Law Legislation and Liberty* (Chicago: University of Chicago Press)

Helleiner, G.K. (1977) 'The political economy of Canada's tariff structure: an alternative model' *Canadian Journal of Economics* 10 May): 318-26

Hirschman, A.O. (1970) *Exit, Voice and Loyalty* (Cambridge, Mass.: Harvard University Press)

Hughes, Gordon, and Barry McCormick (1981) 'Do council housing policies reduce migration between regions?' *Economic Journal* 91 (December): 919-37

Jenkins, Glenn (1981) 'Costs and consequences of the new protectionism: the case of Canada's clothing sector' *Canada in a Developing World Economy: Trade or Protection* North-South Institute and World Bank (Oxford University Press)

Jordan, William (1972) 'Producer protection, prior market structure and the effects of government regulation' *The Journal of Law and Economics* 15 (April): 151-76

Krashinsky, M. (1981) *User Charges in the Social Services: An Economic Theory of Need and Inability* (Toronto: Ontario Economic Council)

Lancaster, K.J. (1966) 'A new approach to consumer theory' *Journal of Political Economy* 74, 132-57

Lansing, John B., and Eva Mueller (1967) *The Geographic Mobility of Labor* (Ann Arbor: Institute for Social Research, University of Michigan)

Lavergne, Real (1981) *The Political Economy of US Tariffs* Ph.D. diss. University of Toronto. Microfiche

– (1983) *The Political Economy of US Tariffs: An Emprical Analysis* (Toronto: Academic Press)

Michael, Robert T., and Gary S. Becker (1973) 'On the new theory of consumer behaviour' *Swedish Journal of Economics* 75: 378-96

Mincer, Jacob (1978) 'Family migration decisions' *Journal of Political Economy* 86: 749-73

Mishkin, Frederick (1977) 'What depressed the economy? the household balance sheet and the 1973-75 recession' *Brookings Papers on Economic Activity* 1: 123-74

Murie, Alan, Pat Niner, and Christopher Watson (1976) *Housing Policy and the Housing System* (London: George Allen & Unwin)

Musgrave, Richard A. (1959) *The Theory of Public Finance* (New York: McGraw-Hill)

Naylor, Tom (1975) *The History of Canadian Business 1867-1914* (Toronto: Lorimer)

Nelson, Richard R. (1981) 'Assessing private enterprise: an exegesis of tangled doctrine' *The Bell Journal of Economics* 12 (spring): 93-111

Nelson, Richard R., and Sidney G. Winter (1982) 'The Schumpeterian trade off revisited' *American Economic Review* 72 (March): 114-32

Nordlinger, Eric (1981) *On the Autonomy of the Democratic State* (Cambridge, Mass.: Harvard University Press)

Norrie, Kenneth, and Michael Percy (1983) 'Freight rate reform and regional burden: a general equilibrium analysis of western freight rate proposals' *Canadian Journal of Economics* 16 (May): 325-49

North, Douglas (1978) 'Structure and performance: the task of economic history' *Journal of Economic Literature* 16 (September): 963-78

Olson, Mancur (1964) 'Agriculture and depressed areas' *Journal of Farm Economics* 46 (December): 984-8

Owen, Bruce, and Ronald Braeutigam (1978) *The Regulation Game: The Strategic Use of the Administrative Process* (Cambridge: Ballinger)

Peltzman, Sam (1980) 'The growth of government' *Journal of Law and Economics* 23 (2, October): 209-87

Pesando, James E. (1982) 'Investment risk, bankruptcy risk, and pension reform in Canada' *The Journal of Finance* 37 (3, June): 741-9

Posner, Richard (1975) 'The social costs of monopoly and regulation' *Journal of Political Economy* 83 (August): 807-27

Prefontaine, Raymond, and Yves Balcer (1979) 'Interaction of labour mobility rates and vesting rules on years of pensionable service'. In Canada (1979c) 2, app. 8

Quinn, John, and M.J. Trebilcock (1982) 'Compensation, transition costs, and regulatory change' *University of Toronto Law Journal* 32: 117

Rea, Sam, and J.E. Pesando (1980) *Public and Private Pensions in Canada: An Economic Analysis* (Toronto: Ontario Economic Council)

Rees, R., and B. Forster (1981) 'The optimal rate of decline of an inefficient industry'. Queen's University Working Paper Series. Mimeo

Sandell, Steven H. (1977) 'Women and the economics of family migration' *Review of Economics and Statistics* 59 (November): 406-14

Saunders, Ronald E. (1980) 'The political economy of effective tariff protection in Canada's manufacturing sector' *Canadian Journal of Economics* 13 (May): 340-8

Schumpeter, Joseph (1950) *Capitalism, Socialism and Democracy* (New York: Harper and Row)

Siemens, L.B. (1973) *Single Enterprise Community Studies in Northern Canada* Centre for Settlement Studies, University of Manitoba, series 5, occasional paper 7 (Winnipeg)

Smith, David (1978) *A Study of Employee Mobility at the Hartlepool Steelworks* (London: Social and Community Planning Research)

Stigler, George (1970) 'Director's law of public income redistribution' *Journal of Law and Economics* 13 (April): 1-10

– (1971) 'The theory of economic regulation' *The Bell Journal of Economics and Management Science* 2 (spring): 3-21

Trebilcock, M.J., R.S. Pritchard, D.G. Hartle, and D.N. Dewees (1982) *The Choice of Governing Instrument* (Ottawa: Economic Council of Canada and Supply and Services Canada)

Tullock, Gordon (1975) 'The transitional gains trap' *Bell Journal of Economics* 6 (autumn): 671-8

Usher, Dan (1977) 'Public property and the effects of migration upon other residents of the migrants' countries of origin and destination' *Journal of Political Economy* 85: 1011-20

– (1981) *The Economic Prerequisite to Democracy* (Oxford: Basil Blackwell)

– (1982) 'The benefits and costs of firm specific investment grants: a study of five federal programs'. Queen's University. Mimeo

Vanderkamp, John, and E.K. Grant (1976) *The Economic Causes and Effects of Migration: Canada 1965-71* (Ottawa: Economic Council of Canada and Supply and Services Canada)

Viner, Jacob (1960) 'The intellectual history of laissez faire' *The Journal of Law and Economics* 3: 45-69

Watson, William G. (1983) A Primer on the Economics of Industrial Policy (Toronto: Ontario Economic Council)

Weiss, Leonard (1980) *Case Studies in American Industry* 3rd ed. (New York: John Wiley)

Williamson, Oliver E. (1981) 'The modern corporation: origins, evolution, attributes' *Journal of Economic Literature* 19 (December): 1537-68

Winer, S., and D. Gauthier (1982) *Internal Migration and Fiscal Structure: An Econometric Study of the Determinants of Interprovincial Migration in Canada* (Ottawa: Economic Council of Canada and Supply and Services Canada)